Women LEADERSHIP
IN THE 21ST CENTURY

CREATING & RAISING
LEADERS OF TOMORROW

by Ritu Chopra

Edited by Lil Barcaski

Published by: GWN Publishing
www.GWNPublishing.com

Cover Design:

ISBN: 978-0-9842368-5-5

This Book is Dedicated To

All Women on Planet Earth

CONTENTS

INTRODUCTION

Humanity is at the doorsteps of the digital world, and we must prepare ourselves and our younger generation for digital citizenship.

Tomorrow consists of a promise and many challenges. History reminds us that every generation and era has gone through surmounting challenges. We are now at the threshold of something much different than humanity's past.

We have different issues of global health then in the past.

We have a different environmental future than in the past.

We have different issues with global economics, population growth, food security, and the planet's resources than in the past.

We have come too far in our technological advancement in every field of industry, science, medicine, education, health, manufacturing et cetera, leading into the Fourth Industrial Revolution.

Yet, we have made little progress in gender equality, recognition of women's role and contribution thus far, coming into the third decade of the 21st century. We are experiencing several regions of the world with humanitarian crises. In our rapidly changing world of higher connectivity but we are very much disconnected. What does leadership mean for tomorrow?

What role can women play in leading the change at every level of society not just in the positions of power?

I contemplated the idea of this book for what it means for women leaders of the 21st century, especially in the last couple of decades. We can see the family structures and business landscapes have drastically changed. Consequently, women now must take on higher responsibilities as it pertains not just to their education but also to their careers, competing for better-paying jobs that are suitable for their educational background, and taking care of their household duties on a daily basis. Their challenges at work and family responsibilities create an added level of uncertainty and a tremendous emotional toll that makes their personal and professional growth very challenging.

My desire and objective for this book is to create an awareness that despite multi-fold challenges we have made a lot of progress, yet much more work is needed to continue to momentum.

RITU CHOPRA

PREFACE

In our modern world, we can only speculate about ancient civilizations and the gender roles thousands of years ago. We can see and explore the history and the cultural and social patterns of the various parts of the world. We can find women who have held many roles, from Goddesses to farm workers. These roles of being worshiped to being exploited are far too many to mention.

In our recent history of the last two centuries to the current stage of the 21st century, it is noticeable that women of the world have played a significant role in the economic growth of societies and nations, from agriculture to aerospace and a whole lot in between. Yet, women, in most of the communities in the modern world, must take on additional responsibilities besides their roles of givers of life, nurturing, and caretaker of the families. The added responsibilities to contribute to the families' income takes a toll physically and emotionally. Yet, women find themselves proving their worth over, and over again at workplaces and in our social, cultural, and justice systems and to be treated equally.

Women in many developing countries have led initiatives to reform societies from barriers that limit their growth process, dignity, and empowerment. Often these are seen as collective efforts backed by political powers to implement these supposed changes. Young women today, however, are experiencing the favorable environment that their predecessors have laid grounds for and built those platforms for generations to come and spreading their wings on the shoulders of giants of the past. We can see that CHANGE does not happen overnight; this should not stop us from making efforts for generations to come.

What has this meant for women leaders of the 21st century, especially in the last couple of decades? We can see the family structures and business landscapes have drastically changed.

Despite the growth in many sectors to provide women with more opportunities in the 21st century than ever before, there are interesting dynamics when it comes to women playing dual roles, seeking recognition, and proving their worth.

I find that the gender roles and subconscious conditioning from centuries of patterns are still evident in our behaviors. Regardless of education levels, skills, and capabilities to deliver, the perceptions and gender "bias" are not uncommon. With all good intentions, this is still a problem for many women to communicate effectively without being misunderstood, combative, aggressive, or disregarded. My personal beliefs are that women as mothers raise their sons and daughters, who grow up to be men and women, and are part of the family unit, community, society, and nation (of course, the modern workplaces). My take on the topics here is to develop a collaborative mindset, come together, and provide a platform of equality in harmony!

The pre-pandemic world we knew has changed our needs as families, businesses, organizations, and economic design. The current ecosystems demand many changes, and as we know humanity will face multi-fold challenges in the next few decades. By the mid-21st century, the prediction indicates humanitarian challenges, including environmental, climate, shortages of food and drinking water in many parts of the world, future pandemics, or warfare.

So, what does leadership mean for the current generations rising to responsible roles not just in the corporate workplaces but in government, educational systems, business communities, and all levels of society?

My goal for this book is to address women of all generations to participate in the collective thoughts to raise and create conscious leaders of tomorrow.

We need to be prepared to deal with challenges we can foresee now, instill values and traits in the next generation(s) to be caretakers of the Human Race, planet, and its co-habitants.

Women need to take the lead in making small changes for the future of our generations and our planet. What we need is leaders at every level in societies, not just in the organizations. Your full potential can be unlocked if you can awaken your primary powers and connect them to cosmic intelligence.

A greater field of synergies can be created when great minds come together, and great minds can generate greater energy when their collective power is tied to Cosmic intelligence. Despite significant advances in science, technology, and productivity, we are still experiencing ecological problems and the erosion of community and family values.

> *For higher ideals to exist in this world, it will require developing a certain sensitivity and dignity for all life. Being uplifted and transcended from greed and hostility is possible by acting through cosmic intelligence.*

OUR JOURNEY & HISTORY SO FAR

Women have contributed to their economies in many ways from agriculture to scientific research. Women, in many developing countries have led initiatives to reform societies from barriers that limit the growth process, dignity, and empowerment. Often these are seen as collective efforts backed by political powers to implement these changes.

Young women today are experiencing the favorable environment that their predecessors have laid grounds for. We can see that CHANGE does not happen overnight; this should not stop us from making efforts for generations to come.

I met and interviewed many women of strength, those who, in their own way, had the courage to pursue what they felt was the right thing to do, for themselves and their families. And many agreed that independence was not a bad thing. It gave them something to acknowledge the hard work of their mothers and be a role model for their next generation. Not all of the struggles have a happy ending. So many untold stories many of us carry inside. We have a lot more privileges than people before us, but the joy of simple life they had is not as prevalent today. Our modern lives seem to have become complex.

In different parts of the world, the cultural values, norms, social systems, and economic means gave different perspectives for women's growth in their respective societies. Women got everything we can imagine. They received the status of Goddesses, were used as objects of pleasure, are the givers of life, and as they nurtured their young, as caregivers, had the patience to serve without expectations. This is enough to reciprocate the respect and caring of women in our lives. The heavy load women had to carry for families' responsibilities, often in unpaid work, is expected from them in expressing beauty, grace, and kindness. As women started to contribute to economies in paid work, and received higher education, fought for rights for equality, we are still facing that battle. Well, in the 21st century, a lot has been accomplished for women's place in society. It took generations to sacrifice and create the platform women today have.

Women must bring their own light and shine their world. For us to shine the light, we need to come out of darkness. We remain either by our generational conditioning, limited opportunities, traditions, or social norms. In the fast race to be treated equally, many of us operate from blind spots. We don't know what we don't know. What we must learn is our own power. Power as giver of life, power of nurturing, generosity that resides within to give before we receive.

There is no denying that, as women, we have failed in the sense that we have not held true to who we are to the extent that we should hold the power that we possess. Man has set the paradigm for how the world works, and we have followed the rules set for our existence. Despite the contribution we make in giving life, nurturing, caring, contributing, the reality is that instead of being acknowledged most women are deprived of basic rights, education, financial security, respect, and dignity.

Whenever we walk in, it's not with demand and assertion before fear, that we won't be admitted. But we come in with fear inside that we won't be accepted. It's not going to be possible for us to make our presence known for long if we continue to operate with fear. For us to be at a place that is mutually accommodating, we need to learn our innate powers and work on collaboration with men. A lot has changed in the last couple of decades in our family structures, in social and educational levels as younger generations bring in their unique set of traits and challenges.

In my dozens of candid conversations with men and women, it became very clear from both sides, women's aggressive approach for demanding equality has not really helped women. Emulating men's behavior has not given much strength but created the "rift" among women to support women in leadership roles. It's been noticed that women tend to behave in a more controlling manner than men. In that manner, they are more likely to be controlled by majority of men. As a matter of fact, it's one of the most difficult things for most of them to be powerful with confidence and assertiveness than exercising aggression and control. The control also meant that women find it harder to gather support and collaborate in partnership in comparison to men in similar leadership roles.

We cannot succeed by ourselves; women need to learn the skills of delegation, trust, and gathering support. It is just a matter of partnerships and collaborations as you progress whatever you have chosen your profession to be. This will be helpful to you and them in a way that will be mutually beneficial in the short and long term. Yes, these partnerships must be established with trust and respect for each other.

So, if you are an entrepreneur, then you are always going to need to look for good partnerships if you are looking to succeed. In responsible leadership, partnership in the form of collaboration is equally important. It is not just up to us only; men and women are both conditioned by many generations. We have come a long way, and still much to do. There is definitely a positive change for millennials and younger generations; the gender gaps are much less than the generations of their parents.

Another area that women as young parents have to manage is self-care. It is also hard to do this when you are raising a family because the children always take priority over our own personal growth. The nurturing nature is often a reason women put their own growth and welfare aside. As I write these lines, I know how difficult parenting can be while managing a career, and for many single parent families, it is just an enormous effort and takes a heavy toll on emotional wellbeing to deal with life's demands and work priorities. It has not been any easier journey for anyone. Generations before us had a different set of challenges.

Questions we need to ask ourselves are:

- Where are we heading as a society?
- How do we need to prepare our next generation for the perils of tomorrow that we can anticipate?
- Do all generations of women have a role to play in raising younger generations to be ready for tomorrow?

As women continue to contribute to the family's income, men need to share more responsibilities at home. Just remember, most men have not been taught to manage households. Their focus for many generations had been as providers, and women as caregivers. The changes and shifts gradually are taking place and we see younger men accept household responsibilities. The lines between the roles and responsibilities of men and women are more flexible nowadays.

And I often ask, do we need to be engaged in competing in order to have equanimity of life?

The inter-dependency men and women have in our families and societies, isn't it enough to get equal respect, dignity and be valued?

Unfortunately, history is full of examples of women's struggle to feel safe in their own homes, free from violence, and have basic human rights. It still seems to be a dream for many women in many parts of the world even in the 21st century. We still need to keep proving our worth over and over.

Financial freedom alone is not enough for women to be empowered. There is still a lot of dependency on men, due to the conditioning we men and women have from generations. Baby boomer women were the generation that aspired to enter the world of work outside the home and aspired of becoming successful professionals and entrepreneurs. Many balanced this responsibility of home and paid career well as they wanted to not just create financial freedom but achieve more.

> *An empowered woman can empower the entire family.*

My own journey of trials and triumphs had led me to experience amazing results despite the surmounting challenges and obstacles in my paths. The strong desire to rise above my circumstances, ambitions, and "spirit of survival" helped me to always find ways to get to the next juncture.

Looking back, I realize that sometimes I followed the paths that were opened to me, and other times I paved my own. Along these paths are the stories of my life that have been deeply etched. Those paths opened themselves to unite me to the stories to be written on the jagged cobblestones.

Each arduous turn uncovered a treasure, an opportunity to grow stronger and be brave to face the harsh realities presented to me. I often wondered how life just slipped away, remembering my childhood, youth, dreams for life, and journey through the jagged paths. How can one get this far walking alone?

After many years of an unhealthy and abusive marriage, facing threats for myself and my family, cultural stigma, shame, fear, uncertainties, and loss of dreams that I began with, my journey was very rough. I was fortunate to have had the education and burning desire to change my life's conditions. I was able to stop the physical abuse that often injured my spirit and my sincerity towards my loved ones.

The question I always asked was, "But why?"

What does the unwanted abuse in a relationship achieve?

Does it just serve the ego?

Does abuse give control over others when a person cannot control their own anger, envy, insecurity, and incompetence?

What's left is broken hearts, injured spirits, and damaged people. It is hardwired into us to lash out when we feel wronged. When someone steps on our toes, we have an overwhelming urge to step on theirs, and it's easy to get caught up in a cycle of retaliation. This is the cycle of abuse that often characterizes toxic relationships.

But is it the only way to deal with conflict? We don't need to return the "abuse" with abuse. Where do you go and find strength?

I was trying to find my own place in my little universe. Life has never come with instructions; we learn and write our own manuals as they fit into our own agenda and outlook on the environment around us. From the dark valleys into the lit mountain tops for inspiration, something of higher value was waiting to come out into existence at every winding turn I took, and it always did. It took an attitude of optimism to see the pieces of treasures unraveling. Then, on the next turn, when you look at the glimmering snow-capped peaks of the majestic and mighty mountains, it's a mesmerizing sight. Then there is its own shadow creating another darker valley right beside the shiny peaks. That's how life seemed often; both dark, gloomy on one side, and sparkling on the other. We, the mortal human beings, unable to fully grasp the purpose of our existence, get so caught up in life's drama and ignore the beautiful treasures that are presented to us.

My story is my experience, and someone else has an equally powerful story. These stories strengthen us as individuals, families, and society through the valuable lessons pouring out of these stories. Stories are woven with courage, humility, perseverance, strength, and staying strong. I created opportunities for myself and paved my own paths many times over. I can recall opportunities for higher education, equality, and ambition to dream big as a young girl. All that was snatched away from me, but not my spirit to overcome and change my circumstances no matter how difficult they were.

At every juncture, I made a promise to myself to do more and help others along the way. Now, as my life's mission has become to take my message at a global stage, hence this work in your hands.

OUR CURRENT STAGE AND THE JOURNEY OF TRAILBLAZERS

The Giants of the Past

Following the paths created by trailblazers of the past generations, younger generations have inherited a platform built by generations of women before them.

Despite dramatic changes in the workplace over the years, one thing remains the same: women are still outnumbered by men in the positions of power. As we look and analyze the data available today, women make up approximately 48 percent of the labor market. It gives us a glimpse into women's dual roles in their paid and unpaid work.

For many obvious reasons, women often take less responsible jobs. There are many reasons for this imbalance, but one of the most frequently cited is the so-called "leaky pipeline." This refers to the fact that women are more likely than men to leave the workforce at various points throughout their careers. Whether it's to start a family or care for elderly parents.

The discussion of women in the workplace has been had many times before. The conversation often surrounds the topics of equal pay, equal opportunity, and the like.

For generations, women have fought for equality and to be seen as equal members of society. This fight has essentially been won in recent years, at least in the developed world. Women now have many more rights than men and can participate in all aspects of society.

Introduction to the History of the Women's Movement

1848 - Seneca Falls, New York

<u>First Women's Rights Convention</u>

The women's right to vote in particular is met with derision by the public. But a movement is born.

1840s to 1850s

1851 - Sojourner Truth

<u>Feminism</u>

In her 1851 speech "Ain't I a woman?", American feminist and former slave Sojourner Truth draws attention to how women experience sexism differently.

1873 - New Zealand

<u>32,000 In numbers</u>

32,000 signatures in a 270-metre long suffrage petition. New Zealand becomes the first self-governing nation to allow women to vote.

1870s to 1880s

1885 - Invention

<u>A two-wheeled miracle</u>

The bicycle as we know it today, paves way for less restrictive clothing and greater mobility for women in some regions.

1911 - Austria, Denmark, Germany...

<u>International Women's Day</u>

1st International Women's Day, more than 1 million people in Austria, Denmark, Germany & Switzerland for women's suffrage & labour rights.

1900s to 1920s

1929s - Egypt

<u>Doctors stand up against FGM</u>

In the first known campaign of its kind, the Egyptian Society of Physicians goes against tradition by declaring the negative health effects of Female Genital Mutilation.

1929 - Nigeria

<u>Aba Women's Riot</u>

Incensed by their social standing under colonial rule, the Igbo women send palm leaves to fellow sisters across Southeastern Nigeria.

1920s to 1940s

World War I to World War 2

<u>The changing world of work</u>

World War I & II drive women to take on "untraditional" jobs as men head to war. Rosie the Riveter has been interpreted as a symbol of women's empowerment.

https://interactive.unwomen.org/multimedia/timeline/womenunite/en/index.html#/1840

According to UN women's reflection of historical major events in last two centuries for women's rights and initiatives, it is notable that the relentless efforts made by trailblazer women in last 200 years.

1945

The United Nations is born

Following the devastation of World War II, the United Nations forms in 1945 to foster international co-operation. Its charter enshrines gender equality.

1945 to 1948

1948

Over 500

Translated to more than 500 languages, the Universal Declaration of Human Rights spells out basic rights & freedoms all human beings should enjoy.

1970 - Mexico

Activists Unite

The 1st International Women's Year, 1st UN Decade for Women & first world conference on women in Mexico escalates discourse on women's rights.

1970s to 1990s

1885 - Invention

A two-wheeled miracle

The bicycle as we know it today, paves way for less restrictive clothing and greater mobility for women in some regions.

1995 - Beijing

Beijing Declaration & Platform for Action

A comprehensive framework adopted at the 4th World Conference for Women with a road map of actions under 12 critical areas to advance women's rights.

1990s to 2000s

2006 - India

The Gulabi Gang: Justice for women

A "gang" of tens of thousands of women dressed in pink (gulabi) collectively tackle social injustices against women in the state & are inspiring similar uprisings in the nation.

2011 - Arab States

Challenging the status quo

Women protest for their rights as part of the pan-Arab movement. The outcry placed women into the global limelight, challenging perceptions of them as passive.

2000s to 2010s

2013 - New York, USA

Education for all

Surviving a gunshot wound to the head & neck, Malala speak as she marks her first public appearance at the UN on her 16th birthday in 2013.

https://interactive.unwomen.org/multimedia/timeline/womenunite/en/index.html#/1840

These efforts led by women leaders were not limited to any one region or nation or culture. The global history accounts for the suffering, struggles for rights, and having their voice heard have made its impact, the younger generations now have a platform to rise and spread their wings. The battle for equal rights and gender equality is still ongoing.

Here are few other key dates related to women's rights until end of 20th century in United States:

1839	Mississippi grants women the right to hold property
1869	Wyoming passes first suffrage law
1890	Wyoming gives women right to vote in all elections
1900	Every state has Married Women's Property Act
1920	19th Amendment to the US Constitution: women can vote
1963	Equal Pay Act passed by Congress
1964	Title VII of Civil Rights Act: gender is a protected class
1969	Women meeting physical requirements can hold men's jobs
1974	It is illegal to force pregnant women to take maternity leave
1978	Pregnancy Discrimination Act passed
1981	US Supreme Court: excluding women from draft is constitutional
1997	College athletic programs must equally include men and women

However, there is still a lot more effort needed. In many parts of the world, women are still not seen as equal to men and are often treated as second class citizens. But thanks to the recent generations of women, the Millennials and Gen Xers women have a platform to stand on and fly their wings to reach new heights. They have the chance to continue the fight for equality and make the world a better place, one of equality for all women.

With the dawn of the 21st century, there was an increase in the number of women in leadership positions globally. Younger generations of women today have inherited a platform created by other women of past generations. Thanks to these women's hard work and dedication, women today have advanced their careers in the fields often reserved for men, making a difference in the world.

With notable advances, there is still a long way to go before achieving true equality. Women continue to face discrimination and sexism in many industries, and there is a need for more women in leadership positions. We must continue to strive for a better future for all women.

HOW WOMEN HAVE LED INITIATIVES TO REFORM SOCIETIES

Women, Dignity, and Empowerment are still dilemmas in many cultures and societies in the 21st century. The barriers that keep women from achieving growth and reform are unlimited. Some common factors are women's lack of power and charisma, the struggles and trials faced by different generations of women, and the pathways to empowerment.

Despite playing a crucial role in society, women have not always been given the dignity and support they need. Even though in many cultures, the importance of women in society has always been acknowledged and they have held the roles of Goddess and Queens, yet we see they have often been denied the dignity and respect they deserve and still in this day and age many women are living in impoverished circumstance and homelessness, facing unsafe living conditions.

But things are changing. Since generations have passed, women have been unable to break through the barriers that have held them back. Power and charisma are attributes they assert and use to carve out their paths to success. By claiming their power and charisma, women can design a successful approach for themselves.

It took many generations for women to break through the barriers that have prohibited them from gaining a place in society. However, this is not to say that the struggles and trials faced by women have come to an end. But as more and more women step into the spotlight and claim their rightful place in the world, it is becoming clear that anything is possible.

WOMEN'S EMPOWERMENT IS ONE OF OUR TIME'S MOST CRUCIAL DEVELOPMENT OBJECTIVES

Women's empowerment means having the power to make decisions about one's life. It includes financial independence, access to education and health care, and participation in the political process. Despite the progress made in recent years, women still face significant barriers to empowerment. These barriers include gender discrimination, violence against women, and unequal access to education and economic opportunities. Only when these barriers are broken down can we create a more just and equal world for all.

THE PREMISE OF THE BOOK

Here are 10 major ideas that are the focal points discussed in the book.

1. Our Successes and Challenges Thus Far

Here, I have considered the history of the last 200 years from global perspectives, our trials, tribulations, and successes coming into the third decade of the 21st century. The changes in our social norms that took place either by need of the moment or were forced upon to adopt newer and different ways of living and working are noteworthy. In many aspects of our lives, we have made subsequent progress yet there have been enormous battles fought to get this far. Those heroes of the past must be acknowledged. Today we stand upon the shoulders of those giants, the foundations they have built for us and the platforms they have given us to continue building this momentum of justice and equality.

2. Identifying the Main Issues We're Facing

There is a significant difference in the amount of wealth and income controlled by a smaller segment of society. In addition, the middle class is shrinking. Most women in their adult years are now contributing to the family's income either by working for other organizations or engaging in their own small enterprises.

Since more influential organizations are making it more difficult for small businesses to compete in the marketplace, small businesses are experiencing difficulties in surviving, affecting employment in particular.

As new generations enter the workforce, the gig economy is taking over, and employer loyalty is nonexistent. We are witnessing the exit of the baby boomers from the workforce and their transition into retirement.

It is crucial to keep in mind that the bottom line is that, as technology continues to replace human beings and corporations become more profitable, we will have to decide that shareholders alone will not receive monetary benefits of the advancements in technology.

The bottom line is the fact that, for a product or service to be sold, companies need consumers, and if the consumer is not able to afford the product or service, then where will the money come from?

3. Crisitunity—Creating an Opportunity in Every Crisis

Among the traits of a strong culture are an infinite amount of creativity and a wide range of survival strategies. Finding an opportunity in a crisis, the original word "Crisitunity" coined by the well-known comic TV serial Homer Simpson comes from the Chinese language, where the Chinese symbol for crisis and opportunity is the same.

"CRISITUNITY" is the ideal term to reflect a crisis and the opportunity to do something.

How do you handle a crisis posed by a seemingly small challenge?

Our ability to deal with these situations depends mainly on how well we are equipped. Most people cannot turn a crisis into an opportunity on their own. It requires a collaborative effort, thought process, and creativity to turn crises into opportunities. An openness to change and an open mind are prerequisites for seeing opportunities in crises. In the post-pandemic world, we have seen many examples of people who lost their businesses and livelihood and turned their crises into innovative services and products for their customers.

As we head toward the mid-century, many significant challenges for humanity are present. Work has begun, but a much more collaborative effort is needed. The business strategies of past decades need to be revised to suit today's ecosystem becoming digital. A good example: taking into account the COVID-19 crisis, as well as the growth of digital interaction; our identities are being shared widely, *creating both opportunities and risks.*

4. Gaps Analysis and Power Dynamics

The gaps and/or power dynamics in my perspectives are not with intent to come with competition, but with the hope of creating collaborations between men and women to come together for creating and raising leaders of tomorrow, who will be facing not only newer challenges that our humanity faces, but also the parallel challenges of digitalization, readiness of the Fourth Industrial Revolution, workforce and employment for all eligible adults including neuro-divergent young adults.

> *We have come far, still have a long way to go.*

5. The Broken Promises of Equivalence

Equality and dignity for human life, in my view, is our birthright. It does not belong to a specific gender. As women, the givers of life, we nurture the embryo until the child comes into the world, then nurturing the child through the infancy, adolescence, and until they are young adults, a mother role is heavily involved. This effort only is worth the respect and dignity women must have. We don't need to ask further to have basic human rights as given to men, that women have brought into this world. I am not taking away at all the role of fathers or men for providing living and financial means to their families, the conversation here is about respect, dignity, equality, and basic human rights for women.

6. Seven Guiding Principles

The guiding principles I talk about here are timeless values that we as humans find so much strength in our behavior, thought processes, living values we adhere to and can relate to.

These Seven Guiding Principles I talk about here are:

1. We humans have several commonalities.

2. We thrive with and among other humans.

3. We seek fulfillment (Maslow's chart).

4. We act with self-interest first (WIIFM).

5. We learn and act with our natural curiosity and perception.

6. We excel in our personal growth with integrity and authenticity.

7. We value and respect everyone's contribution.

Each principle is discussed in detail in the next Segment.

7. Every Individual Has a Role to Play

Every life form in our eco-systems, on earth's surface, beneath the surfaces (microorganism) and in deep oceans have a role to play. This role each life-form has contributes to support other living beings in one way or another. Let's just talk about humans of all strengths, abilities, and skills. As a human population, we need more products, services, education, skills, financial means, policies, protection, and a whole lot more. The list is just too long to mention. There are people here in our times, with different levels of skills, strength, needs, talents, and lack of them at the same time. As cohabitants of the planet, our governments, and societies must provide the basic needs, and opportunities for all to be part of the global economy, especially as we are entering the Fourth Industrial Revolution. We need more collaborative ideas and initiatives going forward.

8. Change Begins With Each One of Us

Despite visible differences, mutual respect is appreciated. Appreciation of others' points of view and the knowledge or creativity they bring into society. There are no straight answers and/or "fixes" for the complex issues most communities deal with at regional, political, cultural, or economic levels. My attempt here is to create an awareness for each of us who is willing to bring forward the small changes that will benefit not just them but will make our environments safer and healthier for a long time to come and for many generations into the future

9. How to Create a More Sustainable Future

Due to the Fourth Industrial Revolution, livelihoods have been significantly affected, and new skills are in high demand. Business disruptions will inevitably have profound impacts on the employment landscape in many sectors, resulting in a similar trend of both new jobs being created and existing jobs being eliminated in equal numbers. Business models have been transformed by the Fourth Industrial Revolution, creating a potentially heightened level of productivity and a widening gap between existing skills and those most desirable by employers. These trends aren't limited to the post-COVID-19 pandemic economies. There cannot be silence when it comes to social justice and basic needs for all.

10. Universal Awareness Humanity's Common Goals

The Fourth Industrial Revolution-related innovations have initiated the need to redefine our kind "what it means to be a human" in the 21st century. Whether it's artificial intelligence, quantum computing, frontier technologies, digital identity, or the future of 3D printing.

With new discoveries being made rapidly that go beyond the high use of voice-activated assistants, on our phones and home devices, the need arises for moral, ethical, and fair use of such innovations, for example, gene editing and memory extraction.

New technologies raise questions about what it means to be human, what personal data should be shared, what our privacy rights are, and what individual responsibilities are; so many needs to be sorted out from all sides; on the part of frontier technologies, government oversight and compliance, and user awareness.

Technology needs to be used as a tool by people, that's by people, and it needs to foster humanity as well as empower. Individuals and organizations must take collective responsibility to foster innovation that truly benefits society.

THE PROBLEMS WE STILL FACE

What people show to the outside world, it's just a glimpse after the personality, persona, struggles, trials, and a whole lot more than that to find out what else they are made of or have achieved. How can their stories inspire others, others who can relate to themselves with these unknown, unsung heroes?

At every stage in their lives, leaders that are just starting out to experience as they have come to the other side of the struggles.

They may not be famous or have a huge social media following or live a kind of life to brag about.

In the last couple of decades, it seems like hundreds of years have passed, with all of the rapid changes in every aspect of our societies, communities, and how we live and work have taken place. It's amazing. We have seen many challenges in leadership not just in government, in companies and how the coming generations view leadership qualities. We are going through really interesting dynamics or forward lives, the fast pace of changes that we cannot even stop, breathe, and make sense of it all.

There are a lot of concerns, many different opinions, because now we have social media platforms at our disposal, in the palms of our hands, 24/7, that allow us to express ourselves, our anger, rage, disagreements, and everything else that one wants to express in the shadows of these faceless avatars. This does not mean that social media has negative purposes only, however, this has become an outlet for those who feel being left out, let down, ignored, or simply do not have a way to create a healthy dialogue. So, it creates many sides then one united and healthy community.

As the information shared in these social platforms has a very short life, sometimes even seconds, and the attention span for average human beings has been decreasing for the last few years only, I always wonder how people would retain information. The information, the valuable lessons that we had learned by reading literature, the literary works of many scholars, visionaries, and leaders of the past who had shared their unique perspectives, experiences, visions for the world and the generations to come. I often find it that our distracted attention, social pressures, and ability to keep up with the ever-changing demands plays on our current lifestyles.

As we see in the post pandemic world, that so much has changed in a very short period. For most of us, in the light of COVID-19, people have had to make opportunities for themselves. They had to be innovative enough to create opportunities for their customers, find ways to stay in their business or simply get wiped out.

Nowadays, it's OK to see women who are vulnerable, share their stories with unknown strangers in order to help themselves and others. This is a huge, big change that we see from the recent past, that was sort of don't tell, don't say, don't share, etc. Experience is a big thing. Sharing takes courage and sharing personal stories of stigmatic nature is now seen to be OK and welcomed by many. The voices are being raised and heard. This does not always create a pathway for reliable advice or actions to take but may help others while seeking help. Our world has become smaller, sometimes just in the palms of our hands that a small device can connect us around the globe. Now realize the power of this phenomena, either good or bad, how powerful this is. We have an overload of information in the palms of our hands, and the freedom and privacy to absorb this overload of information.

If you were born in 1970's or after, you have witnessed several major events such as Y2K, 9/11 attack, 2008 financial crash, a few wars in last 25–30 years, arrival of the internet, eCommerce, loads of technologies in "cloud", a few major earthquakes, famines, floods, and forest fires, pandemics, Artificial Intelligence becoming part of our daily lives, AR/VR, renewable energy, worsening air and ocean pollution to name a few major happenings in our lifetimes. We have seen how our parents and grandparents lived and heard events of their lives before we were born.

> *Somehow, the mundane tasks got easier and life overall complicated.*

Currently, in this decade of the 21st century, we have six generations in the workplace (both men and women). Access to information and technical platforms like no other time before us had. Urban women today have more investment in education than men in some metropolitans, are paid less and do more of the unpaid work in caretaking of the families. Women are often charged more for similar products and services and pay significantly higher prices for products suited for women; thus, women contribute to the economy much more.

Our children today are growing up in an extremely fast paced integrated world than we could not have imagined when we were adolescent. The urban lifestyles of families have become isolated, technology dependent, less time for nurturing the young, as parents spend most of their time in highly demanding careers to keep up the costs of lifestyles. The pace younger generation is living and learning today, there is a vital role parents and grandparents have to play to ensure the future they are moving into is an environment that is nurtured by conscious efforts we make today.

We cannot ignore the perils of tomorrow. The challenges we can see all around us are global health, environmental, human rights, social justice, global diversity, and inclusion as the world economies have become more integrated and products and services are distributed across borders. Access to education, job-skills for young adults, especially in the regions where lives have been disrupted due to wars, natural disasters, and political motives.

For women leaders, the business owners, those who are in charge and accountable for managing their teams or businesses, accountability and honesty is the most valuable gift they can give to their customers or stakeholders.

> *Good news is that we can still do a lot to change the course of tomorrow. Work needs to be done today.*

Perception and Misperceptions of Women

The costs for a woman of being perceived as feminine: we have seen that the more masculine a woman appears to be the more antagonism she will arouse, but it is also true that the more a woman is perceived as a feminine woman the less likely it is that she will be perceived as professionally competent. (*Heilman 1980; Heilman &*

Stopeck 1985). The qualities required of leaders and those required for femininity are at odds with each other.

A research/experiment by *Heilman & Stopeck and a report by Gillen 1981* revealed that the physical attractiveness aspects of both sexes, men and women, as they represent their respective gender matter. An attractive man is considered to be more masculine than an unattractive man, and attractive women are thought to be more feminine than an unattractive woman. It should be a professional advantage for a man to be considered attractive because people associate masculinity with professional competence. By the same token, being an attractive woman should be a professional disadvantage, because people associate femininity with incompetence. Those expectations are borne out by an experiment in which working men and women were participants.

Four different groups of participants were asked to account for the success of a fictitious company executive they believed was a real person. An assistant vice president who was career oriented and interested in advancement. The executive's starting salary and current salary were supplied, as well as a big copy of a fictitious identification card, which included a photograph taken when the executive had joined the company. Each group of participants saw a different photograph. One group saw an attractive man, another an unattractive man, third an attractive woman, and the fourth and unattractive women. All the participants received this same written description of the executive: only the photographs varied. Next the participant evaluated the executive in several different ways.

One important question tested whether the participants' perception of the attractiveness of the people in the photographs go inside it with those of the experimenters. They did. The photographs the experimenters had designated as attractive were in fact seen as more attractive than the designated as unattractive. In addition, the attractive male was seen as more masculine than the unattractive one and the attractive female was seen as more feminine than the unattractive one.

It appears, then, that attractiveness works differently for men and women because it intensifies masculinity and femininity. Attractive men are seen more masculine and therefore as more deserving of their success and more capable than unattractive men. Attractive women are seen as more feminine and thus less deserving and less capable than they are unattractive colleagues.

> *A leader is the one who assumes responsibility,*
> *sets goals, leads by example, has a clear vision of*
> *his/her destinations, is trustworthy and admired*
> *by his/her followers.*

The Cost for a Women of Being Masculine

A meta-analysis of studies concentrating on evaluation of women as leaders suggests that women are at a particular disadvantage when their leadership style is perceived as masculine. (*Eagly, Makhijani & Klonski 1992*). Having a style that is assertive to the point of appearing autocratic rather than cooperative and participative, is especially costly for a woman. In experiments investigating the effects of autocratic leaders, bosses who tell their subordinates what to do without consulting them, women received especially negative evaluations. The meta-analysis also concludes that women whose styles are identical to men's are seen as more task oriented than men (Eagly et al. 1992). A focused woman appears more focused on business then an equally focused man because being oriented to the demands of the job is seen as a masculine characteristic. Being masculine is not noteworthy for men but it is for women.

The conclusions of these studies suggest that being in a minority increases a woman's likelihood of being judged in terms of her difference from the male majority, rather than in terms of her actual performance; her minority status highlights her gender and accordingly makes her seem less appropriate for the job, which seems more masculine because of the large number of men filling it. Evaluators appear to conclude that if women had the appropriate characteristics for the job, they would be present in greater numbers. When there are a large number of women in a job there is less disparity to be explained. That the phenomena occurs at the professional level as at blue collar and clerical levels is apparent from a laboratory study.

Future Growth & Education

Catalyzing future growth in education technology with additional targeted investment, new education technologies—combined with teacher training on how to leverage these technologies to support innovative pedagogies—could offer a host of benefits as well as economic and financial returns. The new opportunities in early education have been sprouting up in many parts of the world, such as learning through play which has been integrated into childhood curricula in some Asian countries. Targeted teacher professional development on the adoption of playful learning pedagogies is being implemented. These new learning patterns are definitely a good way to prepare children for much timely education rather than outdated curriculums which may not be adding in their developmental studies leading to vocational training.

In many parts of the world young girls do not have access to early education.

The future of education also relies on its delivery upon technologies, to prepare them for digital citizenship. Digital communications, social innovation, data sciences and digital economies require new areas of learning, and access to all to support the **SDG#4 –Quality Education**. One recent categorization suggests **five core areas** of education particularly suited for application of new technologies. The research data provides us with extremely valuable insights, that organizations can utilize in preparing their business continuity and talent development for future:

WIDE-RANGING ACCESS: With the wide availability of mobile devices, and especially as high-speed, next-generation networks such as 5G replace legacy systems, students, especially those in remote locations or who would otherwise have limited access to formal schooling, can be connected to ongoing lessons. For example, UNICEF's GIGA initiative aims to connect every school on the planet to the internet. UNICEF estimates that establishing the necessary electrical and data backbone infrastructure by 2030 could cost up to $838 billion, while bringing down the cost of data to affordable levels could require an additional $498 billion. Together with the costs of last-mile delivery—costs for devices, digital learning curriculum development, and student engagement, totaling $46 billion—a comprehensive endeavor to provide ubiquitous access could require nearly $1.4 trillion in investment between 2021 and 2030.

COLLABORATION AND COMMUNICATION: With greater access to learning tools comes greater access to one another. Email, social media, and online forums can mimic collaboration environments similar to what learners would encounter in the workplace. The playing field remains ripe for new innovations in learning collaboration. Furthermore, such technologies can also provide a mechanism to improve communication and collaboration between learners, educators, and parents. For example, apps such as ClassDojo and Remind provide two-way communication channels to share updates, photos, and feedback between learners, families, and educators.

EXTENDED REALITY: Virtual and augmented reality (VR/AR) environments—potentially including deeply immersive learning environments such as an envisioned "metaverse"—can uniquely provide experiential learning experiences that are not easily reproduced in a classroom setting, such as 3D modeling and forms of physical learning. These simulated environments also allow students to operate in what would otherwise be dangerous environments in the real world. Moreover, innovative and playful learning pedagogies can be implemented in these virtual worlds, perhaps even more easily than they can be in the physical world. According to one recent estimate, investments in VR/AR in education technologies stood at $1.8 billion in 2018 but might reach $12.6 billion by 2025.

ARTIFICIAL INTELLIGENCE: AI systems are a key vehicle for directly applying findings from the science of learning. AI provides the possibility for adaptive learning, which tailors the learning content and pace to individual student needs. While AI systems have already been commercialized by a number of companies, and deployed in programs such as HTHT, more investment in this area is needed, including to ensure that AI-assisted learning is producing desired outcomes and avoiding algorithmic bias. According to one recent estimate, investments in AI in education technologies stood at $0.8 billion in 2018 but might reach $6.1 billion by 2025.

BLOCKCHAIN: Blockchain technologies are secure ledger systems, capable of executing "smart contracts" and other forms of online record keeping. Smart contracts could award credentials when learning and assessments Catalyzing Education 4.0 have been completed and could provide those credentials in a secure format to future employers. These technologies are still young, but additional investment could increase the impact.

POWER TO EMPOWER

What Do the Words "Power" and "Empower" Mean to Different People

Power is a person's capacity, strength, natural ability, and authority to exert influence, take actions, command, or control. And empowerment is amplifying an individual's capacity to reflect the person's power to create desired results.

WORLD BANK'S DEFINITION: *"Empowerment is the process of increasing the capacity of individuals or groups to make choices, and to transform those choices into desired actions and outcomes."*

We can see the power in various ways as societies different than others may describe in their own language, which may be distinct and associate the meanings much differently in ways, i.e., in English-speaking populations.

Here are a few words that might present a picture or thought of how the use of power can **shift** and **create** desired results for the benefit of the masses.

- Personal development
- Self-assurance
- Authenticity
- Resourcefulness
- Inner strength
- Maturity in relationships
- Economic independence
- Positions of power in society

Additional components of empowerment can be expressed as:

- Women's sense of self-worth
- Their right to have and access to choose and make decisions
- Their right to have access to opportunities and resources
- Control over their own lives, both internally and externally
- Influence domestic and international social change in a way that creates a more just society and economy for all

COLLECTIVE THOUGHTS

In order to bring our attention to how women leaders of all generations can come together and sharing their strengths and talents, forming our future, and fostering the leadership qualities in the younger generation, I have created a conceptual framework for individuals and communities to come together.

COLLABORATIVE PROCESS

Collective process is the "idea" of the community effort directed for a specific initiative, or perhaps one of SDGs. The community of people coming together can choose, based on their strengths and resources, a plan of action, steps to accomplish the goals, and measure results.

Collective Thoughts:

- Aspirations
- Vision
- Purpose
- Belonging

Collective Responsibility:

- Tools and technologies
- Resources
- Awareness
- Stability

Collective Actions:

- Efforts
- Participation
- Growth
- Sustainability factors

INDIVIDUAL PROCESS

As a contributor to this collective thought and initiatives, individuals can choose, per his/her interest, a common goal and follow the directions and steps towards the action plan.

Thoughts:

- Basic needs
- Safety
- Freedom
- Inclusion

Responsibility:

- Access
- Support
- Competence
- Commitment

Actions:

- Contribution
- Learning
- Creativity
- Effectiveness

Conceptual Framework of Collective Thoughts

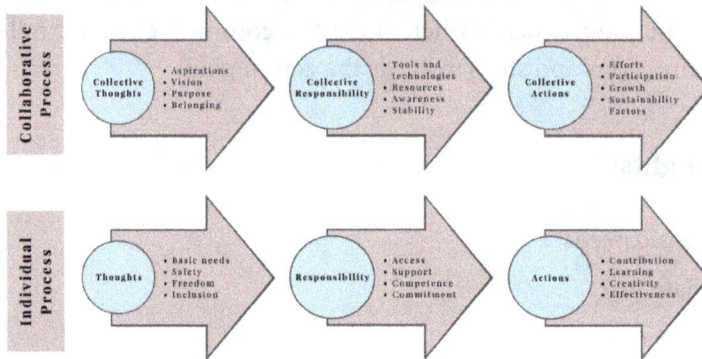

Collaborative Process	Collective Thoughts: • Aspirations • Vision • Purpose • Belonging	Collective Responsibility: • Tools and technologies • Resources • Awareness • Stability	Collective Actions: • Efforts • Participation • Growth • Sustainability Factors
Individual Process	Thoughts: • Basic needs • Safety • Freedom • Inclusion	Responsibility: • Access • Support • Competence • Commitment	Actions: • Contribution • Learning • Creativity • Effectiveness

Collective Thoughts' is Ritu Chopra's conceptual framework for individuals and communities working together and building our future

FULL POTENTIAL EQUALS BASIC INDIVIDUAL POWER PLUS UNPARALLEL INTELLIGENCE

An individual's full potential is equal to their primary power plus their immense intelligence. Developing our inner potential requires mastery over our mind. The mind is the source of all our experiences. Individual experiences are created and perceived through the mind's ability, filtered mainly by our past exposures, personal circumstances, and learning through the environment we grow. Our experiences change based on the quality of our thoughts. If we keep our mind's ability limited, we have limited our creativity and expansion.

We must uplift and align human energies with higher principles, so they are not wasted in unproductive pursuits. The new dimension of consciousness opens up, and when one can concentrate on contemplative thoughts to bring change for greater good. In doing so, one helps their own interests in uplifting to the levels of **"self-conceptualization."**

5 Levels of Needs

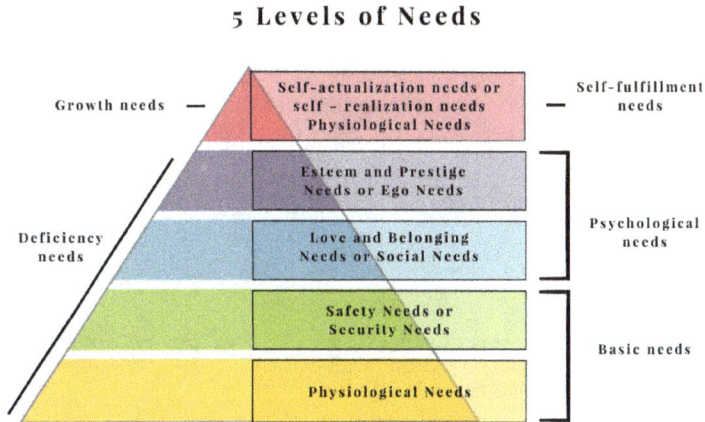

Human potential has exponentially reached unimaginable growth just in the last couple of decades. It has been remarkable to see how human civilization has advanced in almost every field, both in science and technology and in terms of mass production in virtually every area. In addition, we observe an erosion of values within families and communities, as well as ecological problems. Progress has its advantages, but there are also hidden costs. Considering the current state of the world, what can be done to solve this problem?

Since labor management is about motivating people, economic decisions can only be made concerning cultural context. Cultures with strong character have traits like infinite creativity and manifold survival skills, including the appreciation and respect for "dissimilar" and appreciation for the uniqueness of an individual's contribution. Kind and assertive leaders have mutual respect for each other despite the visible difference. An uplifted person with a level of sensitivity and compassion integrated with higher principles makes him/her highly creative.

Among the traits of a strong culture are an infinite amount of creativity and a wide range of survival strategies. Here, we can assess via a candid analysis by looking deep inside and looking back to our history and with an unbiased analysis of our true nature as we function in our societies in our present lives. This can also mean what we accept, deny, ignore, and be unaware of.

THE PROBLEM WITH THE BROKEN PROMISES OF EQUIVALENCE

In this third decade of the 21st century, we see in the business world corruption, greed, conflict, competition, monopolization, and in our societies during tumultuous and troubled times, violence, terrorism and the value of human life diminish every moment. Our current state of affairs is in a chaotic stage, let alone influenced by profit-centered business organizations' greed.

With globalization, the gap between rich and poor has gone up. It has changed the concept of our values and the way we see people. They are just consumers. The quality of life has yet to improve in this century, given that we have so much advancement in food, medicine, and consumer products. The process involved in food production is not at its best for human health. The cost of medicine for common treatments is outrageously high and unaffordable. The distribution of essential medicine for common diseases that can be easily treated is unavailable to communities that need them the most.

We have often seen that most leadership positions tend to be held by men, even in industries where women make up the majority of workers. There is still a significant gap in most organizations' hierarchy of power or leadership roles. Many sectors that focus their products, and services for women also are led by men. However, women have been rising to responsible roles, but their rise comes with a higher degree of effort to prove their worth for the positions and continue doing so. The leadership gap has been explained by many theories and studies, and numerous reports can be found on the web.

Yet none of these published reports or studies satisfactorily explains why those gaps exist, although women are now earning academic degrees at higher rates than men. Not only does this apply to the paid workforce and the professions, but it also holds true for politics, government, and almost every other area of society.

How Do We Justify the Injustices?

Humanity is being reduced to a state of chaos, uncertainties, conflicts, greed, environmental threats, terrorism, or possibly bio warfare. I don't want to say that no one is paying attention or that nothing is being done. The efforts underway are proportionately too little to the hazards of tomorrow.

Few of those who are making remarkable efforts to continuously bring light to such disasters or upcoming monumental challenges are definitely acknowledged. However, that is just a drop in the bucket. So much more action is needed, awareness is needed, and not just the nonprofits. Few kind hearts or a random CSR program is not enough; we are at the doorsteps of environmental disasters. Global competition has complicated our lives with economic crises, family crises, environmental hazards, and human health impacts. We hear about business ethics and corporate social responsibility. However, the average person's quality of life and the gaps between the rich and the poor have increased due to the high costs of living, not just in terms of money and wealth but the family's declined values and quality of life.

Ancient practices that rulers were once taught and adhered to, that remain timeless advice for the leaders of any generation leading the organizations in our modern-day society. These values are the foundation for the organizational leaders or leaders in any role in the society to be mindful, compassionate, flexible, honest, and serve with a sense of service to humanity. While, we often see practices of today's industries leaders to be in self-interest or profit centered. The shareholder value influences their honest and sincere interests in serving their consumers and prospects. We need conscious leaders to lead us into the future.

The Revolving Effect

> *Based on the proven Pareto principle, 20% of the source cause 80% of the problem.*

The split responsibilities of family and work for women, is one of the fundamental factors preventing women from progressing. Consequently, there is less time for them to develop their skills, network, further their professional development, and work on their self-development.

Compared to the years they have invested in their education and professional training; their income increases as a result of their training and education. Family care-giving and well-being still a major responsibility, women are, therefore, under additional pressure, stress, workload, emotional well-being, and physical health needs.

In most urban cities and parts of non-urban communities, women now are taking on responsibilities to earn a living to support themselves and their families.

In the short term, women are disadvantaged because employers' expectations of them and their career aspirations lead to many obstacles. It is apparent that the individual will face some short-term challenges, given the current circumstances of industrial landscape. Nonetheless, the most pressing issues at a societal level are lack of quality time at home, dependence on electronic devices, unhealthy eating habits, lack of interaction and mentoring with the young, cultural growth, and celebrations in general.

> *Shifting the problem where the solution removes some causes but worsen others.*

The challenges we face today, there is not an easy solution for any single nation, entity, or society to solve. *The interconnected web of economies, global health, education or lack of it, human rights, gender inequality, social justice, systemic racism, capital markets, future of work and economic progress are far too many initiatives.* The process to get to desired goals and objectives may take another two to three decades. By mid-century, as we work toward resolving some of these current issues with better living conditions for the human population, we must not overlook that consumer consumption (by humans), at the same time, is causing a serious impact to our oceans, forests, and environment and planet's resources. Education and awareness of such issues can be seen as a solution to minimize the damaging impact.

UNICEF estimates that more than 175 million children worldwide are not enrolled in pre-primary education, and access remains inequitable, especially among lower-income children. While more than two-thirds of countries have achieved gender parity in primary education, it still remains true that there is a significant difference in the rate at which girls and boys start secondary education. Those who belong to an ethnic minority and those who have disabilities can also be subject to additional obstacles to completing secondary education.

A greater emphasis should be placed on building learning infrastructure and expanding primary education enrollment. Teachers must be trained, and a safe and healthy learning environment must be created during school hours and at home. The need for primary education is one of the SDG goals. A concerted effort is needed to improve quality alongside efforts to increase access to basic education. Ways to implement global standards and benchmarks for learning outcomes that lead to individualized learning paths will need much concentrated and collaborative effort. This effort, of course, comes with a considerable price tag.

Billions of dollars are needed to meet the basic education target for 2030 per UNESCO's review precursor to SDG. In addition, data collection and data accuracy remain among other challenges besides funding.

One approach to addressing the problem could be technological innovation, especially for rural children and those who migrate frequently.

> *Progress is measured in a highly visible format that provides incentives to push for more improvements in the areas of focused objectives and goals.*

Violence at home increased as a result of the COVID-19 pandemic. Despite its immediate and devastating consequences, gender-based violence can prevent women from fully participating in society due to its devastating effects on physical, sexual, and mental well-being.

Women who have experienced violence are more likely to suffer from depression, anxiety, unplanned pregnancies, and sexually transmitted diseases. As a result of these factors, healthcare systems are being put under pressure, and productivity is being reduced; it is estimated that discriminatory social institutions and violence against women cost the global economy approximately $12 trillion yearly.

As a result of the pandemic, gender-based violence has only escalated. The health crisis, causing social isolation and increased economic insecurity, made women more vulnerable to domestic violence. Legislation and policies promoting gender equality and punishing perpetrators are potential solutions.

The healthcare sector, judicial system, educational system, and social service providers all need to make more efforts to challenge norms and attitudes that harm women and girls. In addition, data collection, measurement, reporting, and the use of related data in decision-making must be strengthened, and advocacy and action targeting gender-based violence would be supported more widely by community-based organizations.

I filmed a series of documentaries on topics of awareness of gender-based violence and their far-reaching impact for the victims, survivors, and extended families. Dealing with the stigma of intimate partner violence, in many cultures, victims accept this as their cultural norm, and continue to tolerate beyond their physical and emotional strength. The long-term effects and healthcare costs are enormously high for taking care of physical injury and mental health. It draws attention to create awareness, educate and prevent violent behavior, which has much lower costs than medical and legal costs of domestic violence.

Women, men, and children all become ultimate victims of domestic violence. The effects of gender-based violence are far reaching and long lasting. Young children, girls, and boys, exposed to domestic violence have long term health issues and associated costs. The safety is compromised for young children in their own homes, often affecting their education and learning. Domestic Violence becomes one of the major causes of homelessness for women. Thus, an additional burden for survival in adverse circumstances, lack of financial means becomes a vicious cycle for women in such circumstances to fight against.

Even in the 21st century, we are witnessing crimes against women, i.e., human trafficking and much more throughout our modern world.

> *A strong woman knows she has strength enough for the journey, but a woman of strength knows it is in the journey where she will become strong.*
> —SOURCE: WEB

GAPS AND COMMON TRAITS

There is no doubt that women are capable of leading, but, as a woman myself, I feel that women are more sensitive, more cautious, and more emotionally intelligent. Therefore, when it comes to us holding the power seat or if we have the leadership position based on our leadership abilities, women have somewhat different take and skills for the same roles than men. The skills gap or "show" of power is different in various cultures for women. Younger generation of women in responsible roles are more confident than the generations of their grandparents.

According to the World Economic Forum's *2020 Global Gender Gap Report*, there is a necessity for action as women occupy just 21% of the ministerial positions in the world and spend at least twice as much time on unpaid work as men.

Enabling the three billion members of the global workforce to navigate this Fourth Industrial Revolution requires a greater variety of adult training and learning opportunities. Only about 11% of adults in the European Union, aged between 25 and 64, were participating in education and training programs as of 2019, according to a European Association for the Education of Adults report.

How Women Leaders Manage

While it is important not to overemphasize gender differences, studies show that women often lead differently than men. By examining some common traits of women's leadership, it is possible to see how women in leadership positions can benefit your organization. Not every woman will lead precisely the same way, even if every man leads the same way. However, the traits common to women's leadership styles can be highly valuable to your organization, both in terms of employee development and the bottom line in a rapidly globalizing business world.

WOMEN LEAD BY UNITING DIVERSE GROUPS

One of the common themes in women's leadership is a focus on uniting diverse groups. Because women generally tend to be more collaborative, they focus on finding common ground and getting everyone to buy into a shared vision. This has clear advantages when working in a fast-paced, team-based environment. Getting diverse groups to work together rather than compete, increases the chances of ultimate success, and also helps to alleviate conflict. Women leaders have been shown to focus on people's commonalities rather than their differences. In this way, they can get people who are on the surface very different—whether in terms of culture or function, or background—to pull together toward a common goal. This builds more collegial and collaborative workplaces where interpersonal relationships are valued and maintained.

WOMEN VALUE WORK-LIFE BALANCE

Because they often struggle to achieve it, women tend to value work-life balance more than men. Women in leadership tend to create workplaces where work-life balance is easier to achieve, including flexible work arrangements, work from home, flex time, shared functions, family-friendly benefits, and otherwise acknowledging that employees' non-work lives are meaningful and should be respected. Women leaders may also be less likely to penalize employees who take time off for family obligations or who do not work overtime due to the need to care for children or elderly parents, when it comes time for advancement. Broadly speaking, women leaders foster a work environment where excellence is important. Still, employees are not expected to sacrifice their families and personal lives for the sake of the bottom line. This leads to higher employee morale, which can foster greater job satisfaction and employee retention.

Examining some of the **common traits** of female leadership, it is evident that women in leadership positions have many benefits. Creating an awareness of the many benefits of having women in leadership positions is an excellent way to encourage organizations to focus on developing women as leaders.

The fact that women leaders place a high value on personal accountability also helps them to promote a culture of accountability within the organization. Cultures of accountability emphasize personal accountability rather than blaming others for their actions.

The benefits of such a culture are clear and obvious. Accountability fosters a greater sense of trust between employees and management. On a larger scale, accountability and transparency help discourage undesired workplace behavior. A culture of accountability promotes workplace safety and harmony, resulting in better productivity, retention, morale, and an increase in the bottom line.

Leaders need to be confident, whatever their gender may be. According to studies, the strength of their network contributes to building trust and confidence among leaders.

authority
feminine-power Caring
Perseverance Comforting
Empowerment compassion
community motivation
graceful self-esteem clarity enlightened
social-justice
Influence
connect gender Power guidance initiatives integrity
strategy mindset
Emotions responsibility Courage
Giver brave autonomy equality
Warrior authenticity
self-determination confidence thoughts freedom
bravery leadership
Nurturing STEM Shakti curiosity
communications Grace kindness
Loving humility

Access to Professional Networks for Women

One of the most profound barriers to women's leadership is the degree to which women lack professional networks. In recent years there have been more online networks available; however, participation from women on online platforms is low, as most women have household responsibilities and time constraints limit participation.

As opposed to this, numerous studies have shown that men's professional networks are crucial to their success. You gain an awareness of opportunities, get a foot in the door at a new employer, receive support, and develop your professional abilities when you have a strong network.

In terms of employment, promotions, and compensation, those without a strong network tend to fall behind those with one. There are many reasons why women may not be able to form networks for various reasons. Men may be reluctant to network with women because they emphasize the differences between genders. The exact reasons may prevent women from networking with men.

The fact that most women care for their families and are homemakers may make it difficult for them to engage in social activities after work or prioritize these activities. The conflict between work and family often leads to a lack of women in leadership positions.

Most childcare, housework, and other family responsibilities are traditionally handled by women, even in two-partner families. Often, women care for aging parents as their primary caregivers.

Women are under significant pressure to balance work and family and to sacrifice a job to support their family due to cultural messages that a woman who puts her career ahead of her family is a "bad mother." A large proportion, but not all, of women in the paid workforce have children or engage in care work, but due to this fact, most women face this dilemma.

Even in the post-pandemic world, many organizations do not promote work-life balance, resulting in women missing out on opportunities that other colleagues may have taken advantage of.

When it comes time for promotion, this may be used against a female candidate who is seen as insufficiently invested in her career due to family obligations. Family obligations may also mean women forgo meaningful educational and development opportunities that would help them advance into leadership.

Leaders need to be confident, whatever their gender may be. According to studies, the strength of their network contributes to building trust and confidence among leaders. In addition to building self-confidence and self-esteem, networking facilitates the development of skills and relationships.

Because gender stereotypes and entrenched barriers to women's leadership can sometimes prevent women from having the confidence to lead, organizations must invest in women's networking to improve their confidence as employees and women leaders. However, post-pandemic we are seeing higher participations of women in networking groups than men at certain levels. More women are taking up roles as consultants, coaches, entrepreneurs, and in mentoring roles.

▮ SAGE ADVICE ▮

A journey must continue, and it does, either to our expectations or likings or beyond. Women in the 21st century have reaped many benefits from the hard work put in place from past generations of women. We have not arrived at the destination of equal respect, rights and privileges and still have a lot of work to continue. From where we are to going into future, what changes for our work is that we just don't need to work towards women' rights but for the future of our next generations, both our girls and boys, sons and daughters, future of humanity as a collective thought, with collaboration, compromises, and creativity in our thought processes for sustainable planet.

POWER AND PERSUASION

POWER AND PERSUASION

Can you powerfully persuade others and have them do what you delegate?

Learning the essentials of constructive criticism, conflict management, and dealing with difficult situations, crisis management, risk assessment, managing the nay-sayers and bullies around you is imperative. This section addresses the need for one's power and ability to persuade and communicate powerfully. It really matters how you see yourself and how others perceive you.

What Does the Word "Power" Mean to You?

I have described what power means in different languages. Power is a person's capacity, strength, natural ability, and authority to exert influence, take actions, command, or control.

We can see the power in various ways as societies different than others may describe in their own language, which may be distinct and associate the meanings much differently in ways, i.e., in English-speaking populations.

I can list here a few words that might present a picture or thought of how the use of power can shift and create desired results for the benefit of the masses.

CHIKARA

"CHIKARA" is a Japanese word, (a noun) meaning "power", "strength," or "ability" of an individual.

It refers to something a person possesses and uses to influence others physically, mentally, or even politically through the use of something that person has. A powerful belief in ancient Japan was that language had a spirit, giving positive power to positive words and negative power to negative words and that the sound of a person's name can impact a person's life when their name is spoken aloud. We can say words have the power to cause an effect, or power does exist in one's words.

SHAKTI

In the most ancient language of Vedic Scriptures, Sanskrit, the word "SHAKTI" means innate power; in reality, "Shakti" has five facets of power. It manifests as **the power to be conscious, the power of will, or desire, the power to know, the power to feel ecstasy, and the power to act.**

"Shakti" is as though you are surrounded on all sides by the energy flowing out and surrounding you.

You may become aware of the subtle energy as you use it to support you when you reflect on the inner power within you. Allowing yourself to take advantage of the energy as if you were leaning into it to get support.

MANA

"MANA" is a sacred term in Hawaiian culture that symbolizes power and strength. The presence of mana can exist in both objects and people. The belief was that "mana" could either be inherited or acquired through great deeds. All objects, things, and people contain energy called mana, or "life force." Hawaiian culture often describes Mana as a symbol of deep respect. So, we can easily assess that power demands respect.

GREEK WORDS FOR POWER

Ancient Greek, another oldest and richest languages have five words to describe the word power, they are:

- Sthenos
- Dunamis
- Exousia
- Megaleioths
- Ceir

In English, STHENOS means forceful, a name given for the eldest of the Greek mythological "fearsome" Gorgons.

DUNAMIS can have different meanings depending on the context in which it is used. As well as potent, able, capable, and force, it can also be translated as ability or capability.

In addition to its identical meaning to power, EXOUSIA can also be translated to the concept of power in a variety of situations given the context in which it is used.

As a synonym for power, MEGALEIOTHS is the 4th Greek word. Known for its toughness and ability to withstand Mother Nature, megaliths are large stone structures with interlocking stones that stand the test of time.

Lastly, in Greek, CEIR can be translated as the English word power. Given different contexts, this word can be used in a variety of ways.

Above is just a sampling of how the word power can be defined in various languages.

POWER is used in many ways given our abilities, situations, challenges, and the need to use it in ways to bring results we are looking for.

> *A woman with a voice is, by definition, a strong woman. But the search to find that voice can be remarkably difficult.*
> —MELINDA GATES

HOW DO YOU DEFINE YOUR POWER

Where does your power take you to create the influence you need?

Here are few more examples of how power can be used or described:

Command, control, authority, capability, competence, might, dominance, leverage, virtue, capacity etc.

Sovereignty is different than dominance.

> *Command is different than influence.*
>
> *Authority is different than voice.*
>
> *Competence is different than might.*
>
> *Capability is different than usefulness.*

WHAT DOES "PERSUASION" MEAN TO YOU?

There have been numerous philosophical discussions about the morality of persuasion.

Some examples are the underlying intentions or motives of a particular person or group leading or expressing the intent, motive, desire, hope, aspiration, driving force, vested interest, incentives, temptation or reward, consideration, or cause.

According to the Greek philosopher Aristotle, learning the art of persuasion has four benefits.

1. Truth and justice are perfect; thus, if one loses, it is the speaker's responsibility.

2. An excellent tool for teaching, it has many benefits.

3. Having the ability to argue both sides is necessary for an effective communicator to gain a complete understanding of the problem, and

4. The best way to defend oneself is to speak up for oneself.

Aristotle taught the three fundamental ways to communicate persuasively:

1. ETHOS (credibility): Ethos refers to demonstrating credibility or character to your audience.

2. LOGOS (reason): Demonstrating logic and reasoning helps you persuade your audience.

3. PATHOS (emotion): Appealing to people's emotions is one way of persuading them.

How it Has Transformed in Our Language and Perceptions

According to Aristotle, judges are often persuaded by emotion instead of reason, and he was critical of persuasion. Nevertheless, he argued that persuasion could motivate an individual to use judgment and reason. A wide variety of psychological theories have been put forward about the factors that influence an individual's behavior in various situations.

There are many implications arising from these theories regarding how persuasion works in the real world. As we attempt to understand these theories regarding how persuasion works in the real world, because they pertain to the ideas of the mind, it takes us into the world of modern psychology's several branches. My attempt here is **NOT** to get into the psychology and theories, but simply to present a point on our natural human behavior as we go through our daily lives and live through these experiences how we perceive and express them.

Most of the commonly known are BEHAVIOR CHANGE THEO-RIES (BCTS). Behavioral scientists have classified these interventions based on their effects on behavior change of a person. A partial list of these behaviors can be categorized as the following:

- Resulting in positive and negative effects
- Making incentives available or removing them
- Threatening or punishing
- Intimidation
- A change in exposure to cues to alter behavior
- Incentives and motivation etc.
- A goal-setting process
- Consequences impacting the emotional, physical, social and environmental well-being, as well as regret
- Keeping a record of one's behaviors and the outcomes of those behaviors
- Performance rehearsals of planning (self-talk)
- Considering past accomplishments
- Using persuasive arguments to compare outcomes
- Analyzing future outcomes and comparing pros and cons
- Affirming one's role as being a role model
- Assertiveness
- Changing the focus
- Taking responsibility

- Bringing preceding factors to the forefront

From the above list of behavior shifting ideas, we can assume that the influence of persuasion affects outcomes without deviating from the individual's beliefs.

SEVEN GUIDING PRINCIPALS

1. We Humans Have Several Commonalities

We humans have many similarities. We all require the same oxygen to breathe and live, are composed of cells, and experience the same types of emotions. However, many experiences and factors make us unique as individuals. But one commonality outperforms all others: we are all social creatures. Besides these facts, our common connection of loving, caring and being of value is a powerful force within our human nature.

2. We Thrive With and Among Other Humans

We are social beings. We need human interaction to survive and thrive. From the moment we are born, we rely on others for our very survival. And as we grow, and our perceptions expand, we continue to need others to help us grow and understand the world around us.

Yes, we can survive without other humans. But we would not thrive or not be able to reach our full potential. We need others to help us learn, grow, and progress. So, let's embrace our social nature. Let's thrive with and among other humans. As social animals, when we come together, we can indeed find our purpose of being and living.

3. We Seek Fulfillment

A renowned researcher in the field of human motivation and needs, Abraham Maslow, developed a hierarchy of needs theory that the following five levels of needs motivate people:

1. Physiological needs

2. Safety needs

3. Love and belonging needs

4. Esteem and prestige needs

5. Self-actualization needs

Everybody is a part of society. Social groups, associations, affiliations, and belongings based on love and a sense of belonging are essential to enhancing harmonious human coexistence. This sense of social connection gives people the confidence and courage to contribute positively to their community.

Applying Maslow's hierarchy of needs to real-life situations helps us better understand the needs of the individual. As a community, our participation is a critical factor in society's development.

5 Levels of Needs

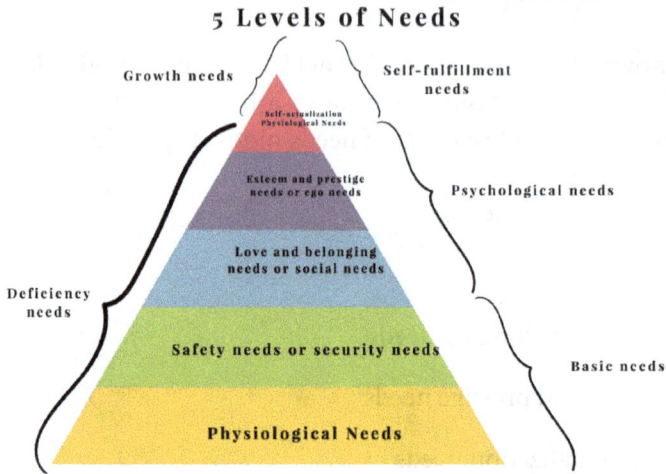

Growth needs

Self-fulfillment needs

Self-actualization
Physiological Needs

Esteem and prestige
needs or ego needs

Psychological needs

Love and belonging
needs or social needs

Deficiency
needs

Safety needs or security needs

Basic needs

Physiological Needs

4. We Act With Self-Interest First

What does self-interest mean, and how do we navigate murky waters of self-interest?

Self-interest as a guiding principle, is used to engage the audience by answering the question that drives most of the decision-making. By answering the decision-driving questions, self-interest serves as a guiding principle to engage the audience we are interacting with. The quality of our interactions changes drastically when there is value for each side involved.

It turns out that a complex set of abilities are involved in this process, which can differ significantly depending on the situation in question. We may see some ethical dilemmas as part of this topic of self-interest. We can explore how social psychology may help us make good moral decisions in the context of those dilemmas.

Generally speaking, it is an influencing factor in our interaction with others.

5. We Humans Have Natural Curiosity to Learn and Act

Learning becomes more enjoyable and rewarding when the brain is curious. Curiosity leads to better understanding. As with everything good in life, it all starts from the desire to do or be able to do something. Success stories are no different; those began with a spark of curiosity.

The field of knowledge is vast; any knowledge domain a curious mind wants to explore. Some simple ideas have become so profound and have benefited the communities in many remarkable ways, specifically in war-torn areas, or regions impacted by natural disasters. Simple ideas to support fundamental needs such as basic living necessities, hygiene, and drinking water have been successful with the support of NGOs. My point here is that necessity and curiosity both are integral to create impactful change.

There may be better ways of time management, life enhancing solutions, or an idea leading to a valuable discovery. There are numerous examples of such simple curiosity-born ideas ending in successful outcomes.

It provides access to new worlds and possibilities. Some studies have shown that curiosity releases dopamine, which is linked to motivation. There is no better motivator than dopamine!

A curious mind can open doors to new possibilities and worlds that are usually unnoticed. Those worlds and possibilities are hidden beneath the surface of normal life, and a curious mind can uncover them. Curiosity or learning is not limited to any generation or location. Our new world of online platforms has made it possible to learn much more than we have had access to before the internet arrived.

> *Curiosity is a valuable asset for humankind.*

6. We Excel in Our Growth With Integrity and Authenticity

INTEGRITY: We excel in our personal mastery with integrity, which is the foundation of our growth and enrichment. This is the foundation of our personal enrichment. Our journey is not a straight line or a ladder; it is a curvy path, and the ability to shift our focus with sincere and kind intentions for the best possible outcomes.

Small steps for significant changes: three levels of integrity.

1. Keeping our promises

2. Being true to our principles and values

3. Honoring one's word on self-first

Keeping one's inner integrity and ensuring one's happiness is paramount. To measure our progress, we must consider these aspects when assessing our progress.

AUTHENTICITY: All aspects of life are guided by the hunger for authenticity. When people strive to align their actions with their values and beliefs, they are considered authentic and act accordingly.

A lifetime of searching for one's "true self" begins with the initial amazement of self-recognition. One can call a feeling of being true to oneself, authenticity.

7. We (I) Value

The importance of values cannot be overstated, particularly in difficult times.

The fundamental beliefs that guide or motivate people, organizations, and communities, provide a basis for social justice and trust in necessary institutions. A person's culture, religion, beliefs, and laws influence their opinions about what is essential.

In our guiding principles as individuals, we have our own set of values we adhere to. They may change as we become aware of specific new facts, changing norms, and social behavior in some cases; nonetheless, we cling to what we firmly believe.

I encourage you to write your own personal ideas, at the community level, or perhaps the world in general, what you value most. What motivates you and inspires you? Where do you see events or changes that don't align with your values? Can you define them?

PERSONAL VALUES:

My personal values are:

_____

FOR COMMUNITY:

My values for communities I belong to and work with are:

_____

FOR HUMANITY:

My values for the world, humanity & all life forms are:

_____

It is not necessary to identify them all, however this exercise gives you a peek into your genuine thought process which is really important to you. What matters most.

> *For leadership at every level, we need to be authentic, have integrity and values for greater good.*

What do you see among those values in a leader that aligns with your perception of a leader?

SMART STRATEGIES OF PERSONAL POWER

Can you create a powerful, heart-based yet assertive message to create the results you want to get. I have taken a different approach to the commonly known SMART acronym here.

SMART

- Simple
- Meaningful
- Assertive
- Resilient
- Transformative

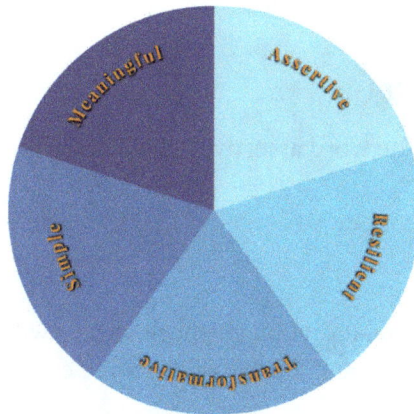

Ritu Chopra's Version for SMART Methodology

SIMPLE:

Connecting with people of different generations in a manner that suits their common behavior and communication styles. For example, Baby Boomers and Gen Zer's have different communication styles. We are often communicating nowadays with collaborative and integrated platforms, and use of abbreviations and

Emoji symbols have become a regular part of expression. Giving a thought to who we are communicating with and how to approach it is a great way to keep messages clear and simple.

MEANINGFUL:

Conversations that bring meaning and collaboration when stakes are high, or just simply building communities and support networks, meaningful conversations leave others inspired and energized.

ASSERTIVE:

When you hear the word assertive, what comes to mind?

Can you picture a decisive person making wise and responsible decisions?

Or do you think of individuals whose strong will tends to overshadow the interests and desires of everyone else?

You may think people may be asking themselves if they are a bit too shy, a bit too humble, or maybe even a bit timid. While nobody wishes to lose or be taken advantage of constantly, people are often hesitant to push too hard, even though they do not want to continuously lose. (This is particularly true of women. Men don't care if they are considered assertive, for men that is considered a positive quality. For women = bitch!)

RESILIENT:

A person with resilience can overcome adversity and rebound from a challenging life event. Being resilient does not mean one does not experience stress, emotional upheaval, or suffering. As part of resilience, one must be capable of working through emotional suffering and pain to achieve their goals.

People around the world have demonstrated resilience more often than we can imagine. Over the centuries of known history, we can find numerous examples of cultures and societies overcoming surmounting challenges.

Some key characteristics of Resilient People can be seen as follows:

- Accepting that change is a fundamental part of life experience
- Commitment to choosing a positive attitude
- Engaging the support of others
- Maintaining a closer bond with a support network
- Personal or collective goals
- A realistic sense of having choices
- An appreciation of humor
- Faith and optimism

The ability to adapt and bounce back after challenges, setbacks, disappointments, and failures is one of the key benefits of developing resilience.

TRANSFORMATIVE:

Simple, Meaningful, Assertive, Resilient aspects can be turned into a Transformative conversation of experiences taking them to the next level.

Transformations are the reinforcements of peace, happiness, love, inspiration, and much more. The minor steps to transformation are simply asserting and confirming the virtues we have developed in our lives. By adopting small changes with wisdom and kindness to our self-growth into our day-to-day existence, we can assure ourselves of the abilities required as leaders, no matter the role or responsibilities demanded.

Later, in the book, I have addressed how to use the above "coined" SMART strategies for Conscious Leaders.

Why Women Leave Leadership Roles

According to a consulting psychologist at McKinsey & Co., a few common misperceptions about why a woman may choose to leave a leadership role include:

- Women lack the ambition to be a leader.

- Women are juggling too much with family and work.

- Women need to negotiate for new positions.

- Women don't have the right leadership skills.

- Women aren't interested in being a leader (anymore).

- Women lack confidence.

The report indicates a message that "the problem is within the woman, and therefore we need interventions to fix her … instead of addressing the root cause.

Most organizations have an approach for women leaders:

- Provide women leaders "one-size-fits-all" sort of training or place them in a "fix her" model.

- Rather than offering strategic career advice, over-mentor and under-support them.

- Leadership Coaching with someone who may or may not have experience in leadership, systems, or methodologies.

- Often, the career path they are given is "gendered" in nature, creating work-life balance issues.

- Higher expectations of women leaders are often accompanied by extra work, fewer promotional opportunities, bonuses, and other compensations.

Women are so often undervalued and overworked. Other findings in this report are insufficient advancement opportunities, unequal treatment, misplaced support, misaligned values, microaggressions, broad return-to-office mandates, and feelings of burnout.

AWARENESS NOT AVOIDANCE

The personal experiences have enabled me to be the powerful spirit to share joy and healing with others who are ready to invite change. *I am there for them to co-create this change.*

> *I credit my outstanding experience with Fortune 500 companies, learning the best methodologies the business and IT environment can offer., solving complex issues of business processes, implementing new technologies and regulatory requirements that initiated many new compliance initiatives, working with Technology Partners and Vendors, Risk Management, Business Continuity, and much more. I often noticed a bird's eye view of the organization's departments' alignment (or misalignment), silos, team spirits, and team-dysfunctions, and a whole lot more. Being in the trenches myself, I gained many insights into common mindsets.*

What we choose, accept, acknowledge, and deny is up to us and we make a conscious or subconscious choice at that moment. There are no good or bad emotions; they are what they are. Shift language, thoughts, and feelings that are not serving in a positive way. First, we deny or "convince" ourselves that it is uncomfortable before we verbalize it to others

Most can acknowledge that the "negative" feelings can be altered; however, our temptation to hang on to those feelings gives us some sort of power. Our capacity to feel powerful and valued in the world and have emotional strength is directly related to our ability to be able to handle both positive and negative emotions, be able to acknowledge their presence, and discern to deal with emotion to the best of our ability, without any harm to anyone including ourselves. It is felt in the body as a physical sensation when we have intense emotions of any kind. It can be uncomfortable and easy to avoid those brief moments.

I often asked my mentors and masters why the bad stuff exists? The answers that made sense to my limited understanding of the existence of everything that we have **Free Will** to choose what is good or bad per our perception. If they were all perceived as good, we would not have valued them. What is interesting is that most of these feelings and emotions inside us are not always present at the surface, they can come and go, and our days and lives go on. Having self-talk to understand these feelings that reside inside us, manage them, and move through them is emotional strength.

I had placed high emphasis on practicing power-skills early in my career as a technology professional. Often my colleagues referred to me as "anomaly" in the IT department. I don't know what it meant to them, as I kept a cool head in complex situations, and worked well with all sorts of people's personalities. As a woman of color, being put in a role to deliver results in given budgets and time, I needed to be equipped to have all stakeholders on board. I often say, in critical, high-stake moments, I found myself either as a "bridge" or a "punching-bag" in my interactions. My abilities to navigate through the emotions of my own and others succeeded me to get the desired results each and every time.

> *"I don't know what leadership is. But I know when I see it."*
> —DWIGHT D. EISENHOWER

THE POWER SKILLS FOR INTER-PERSONAL GROWTH AND EQ

Often known as "soft skill," is a sociological term relating to a person's "EQ" (Emotional Intelligence Quotient). This includes qualities that characterize relationships with other people, such as personality, social graces, communication, language, personal habits, friendliness, and optimism. Soft skills are the ability to interact and communicate positively and productively with other people. Soft skills are also defined as non-technical skills and traits that people need to function in an employment environment. Soft skills complement hard skills, the technical requirements of a job and many other activities. A person's soft skills are an essential part of his or her individual contribution to the success of a company or organization and their own success as a leader. National studies consistently find that employers list skills in communication, interpersonal relationships, and problem-solving, as well as personal qualities such as self-esteem and motivation, as very important and highly desirable. Screening or training for complementary skills such as dependability, accountability, and leadership initiatives can yield an organization's significant return on investment.

Power skills or soft skills are aspects of a person's personality that impact how they interact with others. They are learned and encompass both characteristics and actions.

- They are aspects of a person's personality.
- They are actions as well as characteristics.
- They can promote better workplace efficiency.

These are some key words to describe power skills, social skills, emotional intelligence, or soft skills.

> *Social skills, Graciousness, Subtlety,*
> *Tactfulness, Judiciousness, Finesse, Prudence,*
> *Discretion, Artfulness, Thoughtfulness, People-*
> *skills, Comradery, Benevolence, Goodwill,*
> *Forthcomingness.*

The power in these social graces one possesses is the foundation of personal mastery to manage people, situations, and higher levels of responsibilities not just during ordinary operations but especially in crises with strength and leadership.

A well-known Emotional Intelligence Model developed by **Daniel Goldman** shows how these interpersonal skills become critical for our overall success:

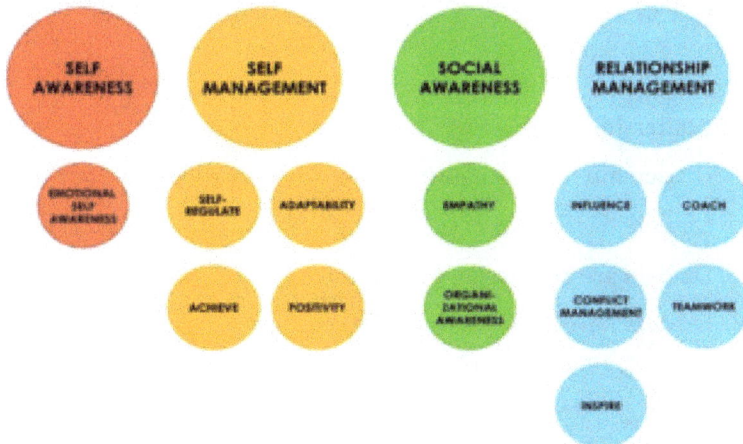

SELF AWARENESS	SELF MANAGEMENT	SOCIAL AWARENESS	RELATIONSHIP MANAGEMENT
EMOTIONAL SELF AWARENESS	SELF-REGULATE / ADAPTABILITY	EMPATHY	INFLUENCE / COACH
	ACHIEVE / POSITIVITY	ORGANIZATIONAL AWARENESS	CONFLICT MANAGEMENT / TEAMWORK
			INSPIRE

Why Do We Need Interpersonal or Power Skills?

The business world today is smaller than ever before. Products and services are bought and sold across many borders. Interacting with people from many different cultures, internally and externally, is much more frequent than just a few years ago. Because this fact is often overlooked, it is where many new challenges occur. A better understanding of how to successfully work in an ever-changing, multicultural workplace and effectively communicate with people is the key to overcoming these challenges. Companies and organizations that meet this challenge create a workplace where innovation and dynamic leadership thrives, and breakthrough results happen more frequently. As we all know, bottom-line results will improve when businesspeople and technology people can speak to and understand each other.

For developing leadership skills and values some common concepts:

- Leaders are created.
- Leadership is everyone's business.
- Leadership is not a role but a responsibility.
- Leaders have followers? Do they?
- Leaders are creative and innovative.
- Leaders have clear vision for innovation.

ARE POWER-SKILLS DIFFERENT FOR WOMEN LEADERS?

ROI for Investing and Learning Power Skills

Every business is looking for ways to save money or generate revenue. Human Resource professionals know that hiring costs are high, not to mention orientation and training.

Challenging times force people to be creative to get the most out of existing resources and talents. This often means that people are asked to take on additional responsibilities that may require customer-facing skills, conflict resolution, or even leadership roles. People who exhibit traits such as rapport-building, relationship management, leadership, and influencing abilities will stand out as star performers in organizations facing such challenges. How can one develop such skills in a training environment? Knowledge is power. "Soft" items are hard to quantify and often based on perception. Even though these skills may be known as "Soft," the impact is anything but: there is a strong connection between interpersonal skills and high-performing leadership roles.

Personal Traits vs. Inter-Personal Skills

Skills are skills. We don't need them just at work; there are many benefits from such qualities outside of work too. People with strong interpersonal skills are better communicators and strong achievers. They quickly adapt and have good decision-making capabilities, as they know how to express their ideas to others, effectively negotiate, and manage conflicts. Personal traits include a specific set of beliefs and values, accountability, integrity, drive, and motivation. Soft skills, in addition to core competencies and hard skills, can include creativity, team spirit, positive attitude, organization, confidence, a proactive approach, the ability to effectively communicate, being adaptive, leadership initiatives, and high performance. Combining what we have learned through our own experiences with learning new skills, we increase our ability to effectively communicate and make better decisions. We also harness the collective energy and team spirit that exists (or can exist) in any company or organization. These steps initiate better results that enhance the bottom line of any business. However, today, this is more difficult to achieve. We often communicate with co-workers or customers who we not only don't see or interact with in person, but we also contend with cultural differences more frequently. This compounds the need to develop interpersonal and social interaction skills with other co-workers and peers... but still, it is overlooked.

> *"What lies behind us and what lies before us are*
> *tiny matters compared to what lies within us."*
> —RALPH WALDO EMERSON

How Can You Tell Which Skills Are Needed?

THESE ARE THE SKILLS THAT ARE NEEDED FOR FUTURE WORKPLACES, BUSINESSES, AND ORGANIZATIONS.

Each person is born with certain personality traits. We develop new habits as we grow, observe, and learn from our surroundings. At the same time, our circumstances and day-to-day experiences influence how we understand, adapt, and learn. By the time a young person enters the workforce, they have accumulated many habits and personality traits. These may or may not serve them well in their chosen profession. For example, someone in the field of Sales and Marketing must have interpersonal skills, effective communication, problem-solving, and relationship-building skills. They also need to work with diverse customers and demonstrate self-management strategies. In a very different profession, a Nursing candidate must have listening skills, critical thinking, problem sensitivity, and inductive reasoning skills, among others. So, how can you tell which skills are needed. Will training help? A self-analysis can prove to be an excellent tool for identifying which skills should be developed based on a chosen profession.

Generally, these skills can be defined in the following categories:

VERBAL COMMUNICATIONS SKILLS: the ability to speak, understand and communicate in ways appropriate to the situation and people involved.

These well-defined methods and styles have been changing in our integrative world of instant messaging and social media abbreviations, emojis.

How do we use the best practice of communications going forward into the cross-generational modern era.

The use of emojis have become a common practice for all generations using messaging devices and tools.

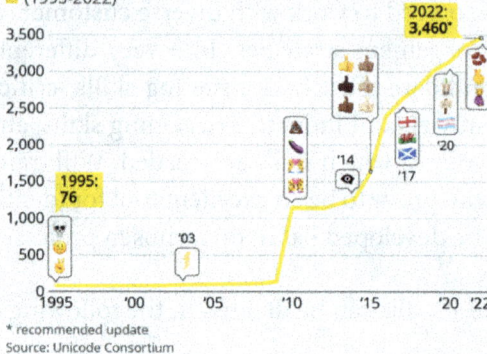

A Short History of the Emoji

Number of emojis by year and release of notable emojis (1995-2022)

The tiny pictorial images aka "Emojis" are so common that they are frequently being used by all prominent business leaders, government leaders, athletes, influencers, celebrities, or anyone with online social platform presence.

FUTURE OF VERBAL AND WRITTEN COMMUNICATIONS IN OUR NEW DIGITAL WORLD

Use of Emojis does not require a proper protocol of written language flow or accuracy, and using these tiny pictorials, users can also reflect their emotions, feelings, or reactions without the use of single word.

More and more Millennials and Gen Z'ers have been using casual writing in business communications. One example I am sharing from my experience, several years ago, all employees received a major company announcement from a C-suite Executive, a very well written page long email had articulately noted the company achievements and going forward strategy etc. However, the signature of the Executive had included the word "**Rgrds**" as abbreviation for "**Regards**". I recall saying to myself, after reading the long articulate message the senior official short-changed his "regards" with only two vowels. Well, these casual mannerisms even in business emails have become common and accepted.

Moving into our digital world of Bots and AI platforms, when users have to do less thinking, and communication platforms generate next words to continue the completion of the message being typed, human creativity is shifting for "eloquent" speech and words to write. I have been curious and interested in this topic of verbal and written communications especially our younger generations. To wish someone on their birthday (a very common message we often exchange with our family members, friends, and colleagues), with the use of emojis, in any order of expressing wishes, we do not have to write our wishes in words anymore. Given the image and just one example, there are so many ways to use the tiny icons with added images, moods, and expressions of caring.

IMAGE SOURCE: BILL CORE (WEB SEARCH)

I can continue on this topic of written communications for a few more pages. In a nutshell, we now accept casual ways of writing even from senior leaders and famous people.

My question here is: How will this affect the learning of proper writing skills for future leaders? Will we need to adapt to new ways of communicating in the digital world? What about the older generations who are not too familiar with new ways of extensive use of pictorial expressions, are we going to leave them out of the digital revolution?

So, this was about the written communications, and I am sure you get the point made here. Let's think about verbal communications. Most of the conversations are happening on devices, not in spoken words. In order to persuade, influence or show their passion for the cause, on the global platforms of integrative technologies, where people from many parts of the world will need to hear these words as we aim for sustainable planet, environmental and humanitarian causes, I wonder how the use of the written language(s) will shape.

> *Will our future leaders express their influence and*
> *persuade in words? Or pictorials?*

Interestingly, there are far more questions at this stage, and results are yet to be seen in another decade or so how the trends of written communications are shaping. In my view, it will be a lot different than the past generations and baby-boomers have been accustomed to.

COMMUNICATING IN FUTURE

As well as replacing text, future emojis could further diversify with personalized (bitmojis) and animated (animojis) versions. According to the few published reports, brands, organizations, and governments will analyze our future use of emojis in real-time.

Those who don't already speak fluent emoji might need to make an effort in learning the use of emojis, as the reports predict the small images will cement their position as a **Future Global Language**.

I bring back similar thoughts and questions; what do we need to prepare ourselves and our younger generations going into the next couple of decades? How will the power of words, or verbal or written communication play a role in Leadership persuasion and influence?

A Rough Guide to Generations

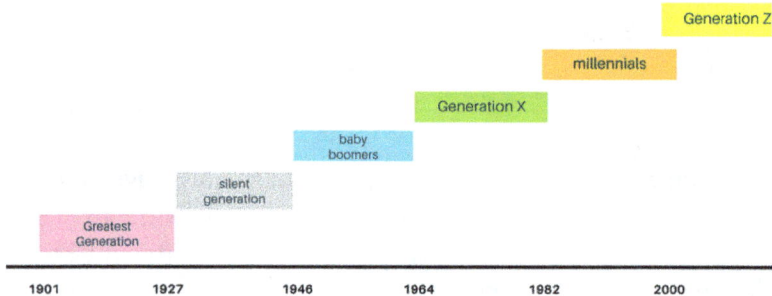

Generation Z

millennials

Generation X

baby boomers

silent generation

Greatest Generation

| 1901 | 1927 | 1946 | 1964 | 1982 | 2000 |

IMAGE SOURCE: WWW.QUICKANDDIRTYTIPS.COM

INTERPERSONAL QUALITIES

As part of the inter-personal skills required for anyone, not just women leaders, the inter-personal skills play a very important role. The inter-personal qualities are above and beyond the academics, professional experiences, and hard skills a person has. These qualities include, integrity, authenticity, self-development, self-esteem, accountability, responsibility, enthusiasm, and much more.

Let's discuss further and how each person can benefit. In my opinion, women as giver of life, nurtures, by nature have some of these in-built qualities, which can be developed further as women play a major role in upbringing of their children and instilling these qualities in early years. This will not only will benefit individuals, but help in creating conscious consumers, conscious leaders, and conscious living for our future to preserve and manage our planet's precious resources, prevent further damage to oceans. Our environment and ecosystem is critical. It is evident that interpersonal qualities strengthen us in our persona and character.

As I wrote earlier, part of 7 Guiding Principles, the 6th as "**We excel in our growth with Integrity and authenticity**".

Integrity

Integrity, as the foundation of our growth, enrichment our personal mastery, I put them in three steps or levels:

1. Keeping our promises

2. Being true to our principles and values

3. Honoring one's word on self-first

The importance of keeping one's inner integrity and ensuring one's happiness cannot be overstated. Regardless of being in a leadership role or not, integrity is critical for being successful in business, and in any role, we may have in our professions. It is imperative, for those aspiring for leadership roles, irrespective of generation or gender.

> *Integrity is imperative for those aspiring for leadership roles, irrespective of generation or gender.*

Authenticity

All aspects of life are guided by the hunger for authenticity. When people strive to align their actions with their values and beliefs, they are considered authentic and act accordingly.

A lifetime of searching for one's "true self" begins with the initial amazement of self-recognition. One can call a feeling of being true to oneself, authenticity. Being authentic is highly important in our communications, especially for those in leadership roles to communicate with colleagues and business partners, and anyone who contributes to their success. Too often, in order to agree with decisions made by others in positions of power, people may tend to comply with such decisions and are unable to speak up (or be true to themselves). It doesn't mean one's authenticity is missing, but here the courage is missing. It takes an open dialogue and consensus of "pros and cons" and what is at stake.

Authenticity, for an individual as a leader is no doubt important. When women are striving in the business world, where they must continuously prove their worth over and over again and aim for leadership roles which they are as qualified and experienced as their counterparts, it has been brought to my attention through hundreds of conversations and interviews I've conducted with men and women from all walks of lives, their candid views of when they have compromised under pressure.

It is up to an individual's discretion to make decisions under those circumstances and situations. It is a common scenario however, where one may find themselves acting against their true self. The following factors further define what else we may include for being "authentic."

Psychologists *Michael Kernis and Brian Goldman* developed an "Authenticity Inventory in 2000" comprised of four key factors:

1. SELF-AWARENESS: Knowledge of and trust in one's own motives, emotions, preferences, and abilities.

2. UNBIASED PROCESSING: Clarity in evaluating your strengths and your weaknesses without denial or blame.

3. BEHAVIOR: Acting in ways congruent with your own values and needs, even at the risk of criticism or rejection.

4. RELATIONAL ORIENTATION: Close relationships, which inherently require openness and honesty.

Self-Development

Quoting from my book, *Mastering Life, Exploring Your Untapped Potential To Reach New Heights*, about self-development:

"One way to deal with life is to analyze ourselves, to look into our own strengths and weaknesses, and make a genuine effort towards **self-development**. By analyzing ourselves, by looking into our strengths and weaknesses, we can turn our frailties and shortcomings into positive ideals. Every adversity carries an embryo of a new beginning. If we take a candid and unbiased look at life, we see that we've learned many new lessons as we are left with memories of past events. The past cannot be amended; it always leaves its marks in our memories."

Self-development can be different for each person at any given stage they are in life personally or professionally. As we move through different phases of life, our need to develop "self," changes.

> *Self-development is ongoing journey, and we must*
> *try at every intersection to have an unbiased look*
> *at ourselves, what we need going forward.*

The external events do have a strong impact in our accepted and comfortable way of living that we become accustomed to. COVID-19 pandemic is a recent example of where people of all living generations were impacted. People around the globe had to adjust in enormous ways, personally and professionally, to suit their immediate situations. To develop inner strength is an integral part of self-development.

Self-Esteem

Respecting and valuing one's dignity is fundamental to one's character. An appreciation or being able to respect one's pride is part of a person's self-esteem. Self-awareness, self-efficacy, and self-confidence are essential aspects of developing self-esteem.

Albert Bandura's social learning theory (SLT) suggests that we learn social behavior by observing and imitating the behavior of others. Albert Bandura, a Canadian American psychologist, and the originator of social learning theory, aka SLT, describes the concept of self-efficacy, which has enormously influenced social, cognitive, developmental, educational, and clinical psychology.

It is a person's belief in their capacity to exhibit behaviors and complete tasks to reach goals. Bandura's self-efficacy determines how people think, behave, and feel. The four primary sources of self-efficacy are mastery experiences, social modeling, social persuasion, and psychological responses.

Individuals with strong self-efficacy:

- View challenging problems as things to master
- Develop deeper interests
- Have a strong sense of commitment to their interests
- Can recover quickly from setbacks

Individuals with weak self-efficacy:

- Avoid challenging tasks
- Believe complex tasks are beyond their capabilities
- Focus on personal failures
- Lose confidence quickly

Responsibility

Anyone in a leadership role must be responsible for their commitment and what their position requires. Taking responsibility for one's actions is an essential part of achieving one's best and self-development.

Accountability

Bob Proctor, a world-renowned speaker said, "*Accountability is the glue that ties commitment to the results.*"

The hallmarks of professionalism are integrity, accountability, and responsibility. Regarding communication, leaders should always strive to be as transparent as possible and as efficient as possible, aligned with integrity. Many women business leaders I spoke with, shared their personal challenges. Most of them I met, have a high degree of accountability for themselves, it was however, difficult for them to make others accountable for their actions. There was a learning curve to gain the level of confidence and as leaders hold others accountable for their respective roles and commitments.

> *Most women are raised to accept what is decided for them as a result of generational conditioning.*

LEARNING POWER SKILLS IS SIMILAR TO LEARNING ANY OTHER SKILL

However, a person's power skills in our current knowledge economy can be transferred to any job, organization, or industry, making the investment in personal growth worthwhile. As a result, these skills enhance our interactions with others and enable us to perform our jobs with exceptional satisfaction and performance.

Power skills are interpersonal in nature and can be effectively applied in many different situations. They encompass many personality traits, such as optimism, and abilities that can be practiced, such as empathy.

> *"I think we all have empathy. We may not have the courage to display it."*
> —MAYA ANGELOU

THE POWER OF EMOTIONAL INTELLIGENCE: WHY IT MATTERS MORE THAN IQ

Most of us are familiar with "emotional intelligence," but what does it really mean? Emotional Intelligence is the ability to identify others' stand and steer our own emotions and the emotions of others.

Studies have shown that women have higher levels of emotional intelligence than men. In my view, women by their innate nature, build a bond with their kins and off-springs at a deeper level, as part of their caretaking duties and frequent interaction with the family members they spent more time with. It is evident to build strong bonds with the proximity and time spent with close relations. My view is **not** based on any scientific study, any theory or branch of behavior science, but mere observations. This does not indicate men do not have the same level of empathy. Our cultural and social behavior may limit them to express the level of "tenderness" women can. I believe it to be more of a cultural norm for women to express their emotions from the very onset of holding a newborn in their arms and express what they feel.

Understanding emotional Intelligence is crucial because it can help us in our personal and professional lives. For example, if we can manage our own emotions, we are less likely to let them get the best of us in difficult situations. And if we can understand and empathize with the emotions of others, we can build better relationships.

Empathy is perhaps the most critical soft skill one can develop for better interpersonal relations. A person's empathy comes from their ability to identify with another's experiences. While we often think of empathy only in identifying with someone's pain or negative experience, we can apply empathy in various situations.

Our ability to develop empathy allows us to imagine ourselves in other people's shoes, respond to others, and vicariously experience others' emotions. The demonstration of empathy helps us build relationships with others and promote teamwork or other goals that can be shared.

The ability to empathize also facilitates stronger interpersonal relationships among team members and colleagues, which is just as important as sharing goals or complementing skills when it comes to reaching a goal. Additionally, empathy contributes to the development of strong interpersonal relationships between colleagues and team members, which is as crucial when it comes to achieving a goal as it is when it comes to complementary skills.

Emotional Intelligence is the competence to recognize and manage our feelings, so they are expressed appropriately. Exercising emotional Intelligence helps to create harmonious, productive relationships.

There are four critical components of Emotional Intelligence:

- SELF-AWARENESS: The talent to recognize our own feelings and justifications
- SELF-DISCIPLINE: The ability to describe one's feelings appropriately (or not be able to describe)
- SOCIAL AWARENESS: Our capacity to recognize the feelings and needs of others, as well as the norms of a given situation, constitutes social awareness
- SOCIAL CONNECTIONS: Our power to relate effectively to others, be able to listen to them and their point of view, these skills make up our Emotional Intelligence Quotient (EQI).

> *Emotional intelligence is the ability to recognize our emotions and express them appropriately and are critical to developing strong soft skills.*

SELF-AWARENESS IS KEY FOR CONSCIOUS LEADERS

Self-awareness, self-efficacy, and self-confidence are essential aspects of developing self-esteem. For anyone, especially in positions of power, when they must make critical decisions that impact the organization's strategic and business goals and their human capital in general, it's imperative for a conscious leader to have self-esteem. Self-esteem, as an integral part of self-awareness, is the combination of knowing and trusting one's own reasons, emotions, choices, and abilities and being aware of the impact and outcomes of the decisions one makes.

Boost Your Self-Awareness

The conscious leaders know that we can only understand reality by considering our experiences through consciousness. Books and school do not teach us much about consciousness. We change ourselves and our surroundings by being aware of our actions and behaviors. We must be mindful of our communication and how our behaviors can affect others.

To boost one's self-awareness, one must understand there are many hidden conversations taking place. External circumstances and known experiences can play tricks in making the right choices. It will benefit from understanding any deceptive thoughts and attempting to look at facts separately, unattached from their own opinion, will help.

LIMITING SELF-DECEPTION

Self-deception is commonly used to hide something from us or prevent us from accepting something. We try to make ourselves believe whatever we want and alter the facts. For instance, we can deceive ourselves by thinking that our presentation was the best in the group or by assuming that people are talking about us when we walk away. It can affect our relationships with others and give people the wrong impression. One of the simplest ways to prevent this type of deception is to be direct. Always say what you mean. Avoid using alternate meanings or phrases that may deceive others.

When taking in information, review it before drawing conclusions. For instance, your presentation may have been outstanding, but do not assume it was the best in the group. While you are encouraged to build confidence and esteem by believing in yourself or believing you know what is best, there is no advantage to deceiving anyone.

We often need to remember that one of the tools we can use to increase self-awareness is to ask for feedback from those around us. It doesn't have to be lengthy or complicated and can be done professionally or casually. The people around us see our routine actions and behaviors and can offer an honest opinion. The thought of asking someone to share their opinions and ideas about us may seem unnerving and even downright scary, but their advice and ideas can prove invaluable.

When asking for feedback, the most important thing to remember is to prepare yourself for what you may hear. Not all feedback will be positive. Take the advice and tips offered as tools to help you improve. Don't be defensive or angry just because the person delivering the feedback may have said something you don't want to hear.

BE OPEN TO CHANGE

We are creatures of habit, and when things don't go our way, we tend to internalize and take things personally. Being open to change allows us to adapt to new surroundings and situations and helps us grow. Changing our attitude can help determine how we build our connections. Sometimes, after receiving feedback from our peers, we may need to change how we do things or behave in a group. Perhaps after a meeting, we must change how we plan our presentations. Whatever the reason, it is essential to not disregard the importance of change and turn a blind eye to its prospects. Changing how we see ourselves and the people surrounding us can positively impact our attitudes and help build better relationships with our peers.

Tips for accepting change:

• Determine how the change can benefit you.

• Don't assume a need for change is negative.

• Recognize that change is a chance for improvement.

REFLECT ON YOUR ACTIONS

While feedback from other people can be a great tool, personal feedback can be just as valuable. Being reflective allows us to learn from our experiences (even our mistakes) and recognize learning opportunities. By reflecting on our actions, we can see firsthand what steps we took, how they played out, and what effect they had on people. Use all of your senses to recreate an experience in your mind and the actions that you took. What behaviors did you exhibit? What did you feel at the time? What type of reactions did you receive from other people?

Reflect on any body language cues you may have used and note any cues you may have seen in others. What intuitions or gut feelings do you feel from experience? Do you feel as though you have learned anything new from experience? These steps can help you reflect on your actions and increase your self-awareness and awareness of others.

POWER OF INFLUENCE

Robert B. Cialdini, Ph.D. once said, "It is through the influence process that we generate and manage change." In his studies, he outlined five universal principles of influence, which are useful and effective in a wide range of circumstances.

- Reciprocation
- Commitment
- Authority
- Social Validation
- Friendship

The influence or a lasting impact a **conscious leader** can make to the society rest upon several factors:

- Stay committed to their vision

- A leader with conscientious attitude enhanced by a gracious mindset

- A conscious leader possesses an innate sense of social justice and compassion for human life

- They are Intelligent, still willing to learn

- Commitment to innovation balanced by a realistic view of the situation

- Their ability to control one's emotions while identifying them

- Listening with a strong sense of communication

- Maintaining a strong sense of rules and flexible when situation demands

- Leading by example but with a sense of duty to your followers

> *Conscious leader understands that to transform themselves from the inside out, they must transform their relationship with who they used to be and what they want to be.*

Each day you are influenced by the actions of others; whether you are aware of it or not, you are manipulated and persuaded to comply with requests by people who, naturally or through mastery, have developed tools of influence. The power of influence is another power skill to identify the methods of an in-depth knowledge of how to use these skills to your advantage and increase your influencing ability.

The aim of learning these skills is to understand how people are influenced and to develop practical methods of applying these in your work environment. In a nutshell, the power to influence is a critical skill for any type of communication, either verbal or written, and communicating anywhere, anytime.

Here are a few key outcomes that influence communication can achieve:

- Understand the "human shortcut" and why it makes influence possible
- Explain the six principles of influencing and how they are used
- Identify critical situations where you can apply the influencing principles in your own environment
- Follow an action plan for influencing success
- As soon as we make a decision or put forward a stand, we will face personal and interpersonal pressures to follow through on our commitment
- Consistency is probably a learned (as opposed to innate) attribute. It is highly valued
- We strive to behave in ways that are consistent with our values and principles
- We similarly strive to avoid being perceived as inconsistent.

Communications: Anywhere, Anytime, and with Anyone

The majority of our day is spent communicating with others. It could be the way you speak in the boardroom, the amount of attention you give to your spouse or the look you give to others; it all means something. Your profession may require you to handle inquiries and build and maintain relationships with your clients effectively.

Here are few tools and techniques to successfully handle challenging situations by communicating effectively:

- Understand what communication is
- Identify ways that communication can happen
- Identify barriers to communication and how to overcome them
- Develop their non-verbal and paraverbal communication skills
- Listen actively and effectively
- Ask good questions
- Use appreciative inquiry as a communication tool
- Adeptly converse and network with others

Furthermore, become familiar with the various methods of communication and learn how to use them effectively:

- Have your "technical" instructions understood by "non-technical" people.
- Negotiate for the things you need positively.
- Avoid misunderstandings from communicational errors.
- Build solid interpersonal connections in the workplace.
- Assess the impact of verbal and non-verbal impacts of communication.
- Earn respect from your co-workers and managers.

For leaders among younger generations of women, these are even more critical skills to have, as they are uniquely in position to mentor Gen Xers and report to older generations in the workplace and elsewhere. As we are witnessing the many generations with their own distinct abilities to communicate and lead, women in emerging leadership roles need to put in extra effort to be able to communicate differently for all various generations and styles.

Adaptability and Flexibility

Being adaptable means, a person can easily change or adapt to the times or have the ability or willingness to change to suit different conditions. Change is inevitable, but adaptability increases your capacity to cope.

Adaptability is necessary for an ever-changing work environment. As opposed to wasting your energy trying to change your circumstances. By transforming yourself right from the inside, you will always be able to thrive no matter what your possibility is. An adaptable leader will thrive in the workplace and can keep up with moving priorities and external circumstances.

For a leader how adaptability shows up:

- Team's attitude is a mirror of leader's attitude
- Feelings about innovation and change
- Enhanced interpersonal relationships
- Training and development are necessary
- Attitudes are contagious
- Environment of growth

EMPATHY IN THE ERA OF ARTIFICIAL INTELLIGENCE

Developing empathy allows us to imagine ourselves in another person's shoes, respond to others, and vicariously experience others' emotions. When we demonstrate empathy, we create connections, which can help build teamwork or create shared goals.

The Factors that Lead to Empathy

Empathy is one of our greatest interpersonal skills because it allows for better communication with people around us and increases our understanding of others.

We are reminded that AI-based technologies can fully measure humans' empathy nowadays. The value and importance of practicing empathy cannot be ignored, especially for those in leadership roles. Studies and experiences have shown that women have higher levels of empathy. Our nurturing nature or DNA gives us this ability. Banking upon our innate nature, women as conscious leaders can successfully create collaborative environments when gender gaps exist.

Developing empathy allows us to imagine ourselves in another person's shoes, respond to others, and vicariously experience others' emotions. When we demonstrate empathy, we create connections, which can help build teamwork or make shared goals.

"Empathy" has recently been given much attention as the world battled with the COVID-19 pandemic, and life seemed to come to a standstill. The pandemic and the integrative and collaborative AI-based technology platforms coming into workplaces, measuring human empathy, present new challenges that we will need to figure out. The leaders of tomorrow must address the humanity of people and the interactions of smart machines.

Here are some factors in developing empathy:

LISTENING AND PAYING ATTENTION

Listening is different from hearing. Listening is considered a skill, so like any other skill, it must be honed. Listening allows an understanding of what a person is talking about. Building better listening skills starts with paying attention when someone speaks and actively listening to what they are saying. Face them and make eye contact. Turn off any cell phones or pagers or remove any item that distracts you and makes you lose focus. You'll find that you will retain more of what is being said. Paying attention and developing better listening skills show respect for the other person and build rapport.

Tips for better listening skills:

- Remove any distractions
- Make eye contact
- Nod your head periodically
- Ask for follow-up details or information
- Ask the person to repeat anything you may have missed

BEING KIND TO EACH OTHER

No matter how often we hear the old phrase "Don't judge people" or "It's not our place to judge," we are more than likely to find ourselves doing it. Whether subconsciously or not, we still judge those around us based on our filters, unconscious biases, or judgments.

Judging can create barriers. Every person has an "inside person" and an "outside person." We see the outside person daily and form opinions without seeing everything. Let's not forget that there is an "inside person" who may be quite different from what you see on the outside.

SHIFTING YOUR VIEW

Being empathic is seeing things from someone else's perspective. When communicating with another person, imagine yourself in their situation and do what they need to do. Shifting your view does not mean that you have to entirely give up your opinions and thoughts; just take a few minutes to reflect on the actions and words of another person and picture yourself in their situation. Putting yourself in their role and analyzing how you would manage the same task or situation may help you express your thoughts differently.

Connect with others by showing empathy and creating meaningful relationships, especially with colleagues or business partners who may have been raised in different cultures.

BEING HONEST WITH YOUR EMOTIONS

It is never a good idea to conceal emotions or feelings. However, this is common in the business world in many parts of the Western hemisphere to not express emotions. Expressing emotions does not indicate being out of control or aggressive but being able to express if any situation might conflict with someone's values or beliefs or is simply unjust or unfair.

Many women in responsible roles, whom I spoke with, have shared their challenges in being able to speak up. To agree to something against values and beliefs does not create a sense of belonging. For women to be in responsible and leadership roles, expressing themselves is still not part of our business cultures.

PERSONAL MASTERY

Personal mastery is one of my key areas of Coaching for emerging leaders of younger leaders. Most of them have grown with technology and devices since their early education, and in recent years have made heavy use of integrative technologies, devices, and platforms at homes and work. The shifting norms of living and doing business have a far-reaching impact not just for themselves, but with everyone they interact globally with, their colleagues, customers, vendors, suppliers, and everyone else they communicate with.

As mentioned earlier, our verbal and written languages are becoming more casual and pictorial. Using Artificial Intelligence and Algorithm generated prompts, we slowly lose our ability to think in creative ways. Creating a mastery of any subject requires consistent practice and honing of the skills we aim to master. My interests in this field of personal empowerment, power skills, emotional intelligence, and self-development for over 20 plus years, I have developed several courses, workshops, and programs.

> *The best part of my experiences has been that many of my colleagues approached me with their personal challenges. When I asked, the answers I got were because they trusted me. I am always in gratitude for those who placed their trust in my abilities and confided in me.*

My curiosity that led me into this area was around the early 2000's. I have numerous opportunities to attend many leadership seminars and trainings, and often observed participants' behavior and their engagement. As a technologist, my interaction with peers globally was often online. I experienced unexpected success utilizing what I learned from colleagues across borders. It is fair to say the curiosity I had was not due to my professional role, but inherent curiosity to understand people. This journey of "curiosity" has led me to develop many workshops, tools, and programs over the years.

> *In my view, leadership does not come with a title. Anyone, rising to the occasion, doing their best, taking charge of situations, and able to do what is needed, is also a part of the qualities of leader.*

My message for emerging leaders, especially women, is to be fully in control of their role and responsibilities, personal and professional. The benefit of our integrative world is to leverage it in the best ways possible, most importantly be authentic to their true self of their own ambitions, abilities, and path they choose. Women, as part of their rise and demand for equality, have achieved a lot that comes with a cost. Added responsibilities of work and caretaking for the families, often have taken toll on their self-development.

Personal Mastery Model

The Personal Mastery Model has Five Key traits among others and inter-relation of these traits in shaping of the mastery skills is imperative. The five key areas are:

- Assertiveness
- Self-confidence
- Foresightedness
- Gratitude
- Inner strength

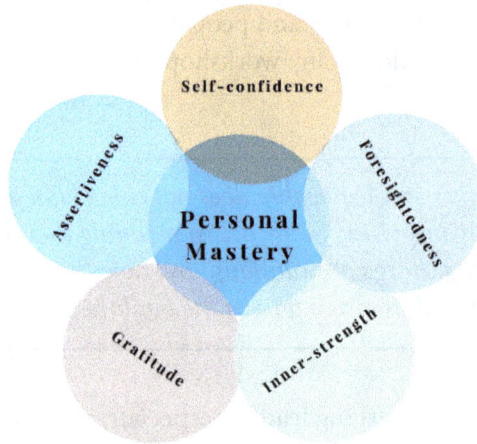

Application of Assertiveness

We all have situations in our personal lives where being assertive helps us achieve our goals. Now we'll continue each practice with the opportunity to develop assertive responses. Standing up for yourself will translate into success throughout your personal and professional lives. It will help grow a person's self-confidence and make the challenges that we encounter every day that much quicker to overcome.

Recognize the type of thinking based on the following statement: As the thinker, you believe things are how you feel about them.

- Personalization
- Emotional reasoning
- Mind reading
- Global labeling

Recognize the filtering type of thinking:

- As the thinker, you pay attention selectively to the negative, disregarding the positive
- As the thinker, you realize you will get the answer through meditation
- As the thinker, you group things into absolute, black-and-white categories, assuming that you must be perfect, or you are worthless
- As the thinker, you feel that you have total responsibility for everybody and everything

PERSONAL SWOT ANALYSIS WORKSHEET

STRENGTHS	WEAKNESSES
What are your strong points?	*Where do you get stopped?*
What do you do well?	*Where can you improve?*
What strong points others see as your strengths?	*What others see as your weaknesses?*
What resources do you think you have?	*Where do you think you have not enough resources?*

OPPORTUNITIES	THREATS
What are the opportunities you have around you?	*What threat do your weaknesses show?*
How can you utilize your strengths into new opportunities?	*What do you think can harm you?*
What other untapped potential can you see in you?	*How are other people in your circle doing?*
	Are there any insecurities holding you back?

OBSTACLES IN ASSERTIVENESS

Obstacles are encountered every day of our lives, but what we do and how we react during these events will determine the outcomes of such events. Our reactions to these obstacles will determine if the situation becomes a minor annoyance or a significant event.

Overreacting to a slight irritant can magnify the issue and make it more significant than it actually is.

These types of reactions should be kept in check; what is an appropriate response to each obstacle we encounter? Like many things, the barrier will determine the answer.

- Overgeneralization
- Polarized Thinking
- Self-blame
- Personalization
- Emotional Reasoning

Negative thinking is the process of thinking negatively rather than positively. Positive thinking requires effort, while negative thinking is uninvited and happens quickly.

Growing up in a happy and positive environment, where people value success and self-improvement, will have a much easier time thinking positively. One who was brought up in a poor or difficult situation will probably continue to expect difficulties and failure.

Negative thoughts center on the individual, others, and the future. Negative thinking causes problems such as depression, pessimism, and anxiety.

Identifying Your Worth

Worth is "sufficiently good, important, or interesting to justify an action."

Confident people exude a sense of self-worth. It gives them a sense of control over their destiny and makes them happy. You can estimate your self-worth by analyzing multiple factors in your life. Take a self-concept inventory.

The feeling of worth can be maintained through positivity, which is a leading factor in one's self-confidence. Keeping a positive attitude gives you incredible power when it comes to self-talk and recognizing and using your strengths. Everyone inevitably has weaknesses, but being positive will help you identify them, eliminate them, and improve them.

ATTRIBUTE	DESCRIPTION
PHYSICAL APPEARANCE	*Height, weight, facial appearance, skin, hair, style of dress, body areas*
HOW YOU RELATE TO OTHERS	*Co-workers, friends, family, and strangers in social settings*
PERSONALITY	*Positive and negative personality traits*
HOW OTHER PEOPLE SEE YOU	*Positive and negative perceptions, as viewed by others*
PERFORMANCE AT WORK OR SCHOOL	*How you handle major tasks*

RECOGNIZE THE DESCRIPTION FOR THE FOLLOWING ATTRIBUTE: **Performance of the daily tasks of life.**

- How you reason and solve problems, your capacity for learning and creativity, your knowledge, wisdom, insights
- How do you handle health, hygiene, maintenance of your living environment, food preparation, caring for children or parents

- How you handle significant tasks
- Positive and negative personality traits

Life's trials and tribulations and seemingly never-ending battles made me feel I did not fully acknowledge my self-worth in many trying periods. Even with all of the adverse situations that I have faced and all of the successes I have achieved, I believe being afraid is a natural reaction when we have been beaten up. These are the moments when you need to go deep inside your heart and have these conversations with yourself. Often called a "self-talk", they can be convincing, and what and where you focus. Many strong women who have emerged from generations of traumatic experiences, had these "self-talks" either positive or negative.

I urge you to take a look at your own self-talks, and what is lurking there in these words we keep repeating to ourselves.

The ability to acknowledge, validate, and apply your full potential is facilitated by positive self-talk.

Also called affirmations (to make something firm), positive self-talk serves as your accomplishment scale. Below are some tips for positive self-talk:

- Describe what exists today in the present tense.
- Do what you want instead of affirming what you do not wish to.
- Self-talk should remain personal; it needs to be related to you alone.
- Keep sentences short and straightforward.
- Go with your gut. If it "clicks," then say it. Self-talk should feel optimistic, expanding, freeing, and supportive.

- Focus on new things rather than changing what is.
- Act "as if;" permit yourself to believe the idea is true now.

If self-talk is new to you, it is a good idea to first think about the things that are wonderful about you, such as:

- I have someone I love, and we enjoy spending time together.
- I am a mother or father, fulfilled in this role and feel blessed.
- My career is challenging and fulfilling.
- When I learn something new, I feel proud.
- I am worthwhile because I breathe and feel; I am aware of my existence.
- When I feel pain, I love and try to survive. I am a good person.

> *Mastery over mind is necessary precondition to discover and unfold your inner potential*

PROBLEM-SOLVING SKILLS

The individual who is best able to solve the problem effectively is the one who first recognizes that the problem exists. Then, being able to focus on possible causes, finds a viable solution, implements the resolution, and prevents such issues from occurring again.

According to the World Economic Forum Report, **Problem-solving skills** are among the top skills, followed by **Self-management, Working with people, and Technology use and development** required for tomorrow's workplace.

The Future of Jobs Report 2020 report by 2025, new jobs will emerge, as well as jobs that will be lost due to the shift from humans to machines in the division of labor.

It is expected that 50% of workers will require re-skilling by 2025. The report further notes, "As a result of the twin forces of the Fourth Industrial Revolution and the COVID-19 recession, day-to-day digitalization has leaped forward, with a large-scale shift to remote working and e-commerce, driving a surge in work-from-home arrangements and a new marketplace for remote work. However, it has also brought about significant well-being challenges as workers have struggled to adapt to new ways of work over a short period of time."

A problem can be defined as a scenario in which the current situation does not match the desired situation or anytime actual performance does not match expectations. Other labels for a problem include challenges or opportunities, crisis or any situation or circumstance for which there is room for improvement.

Future

Impact

Innovation

Problem solving

Crisis management

Level of
productivity

Past

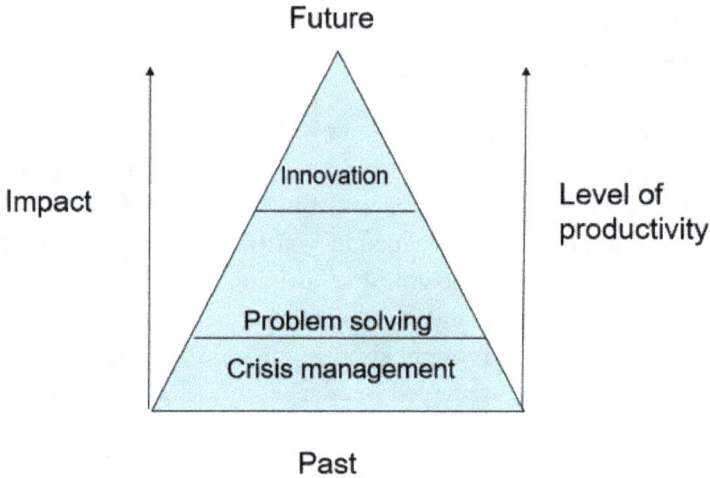

Creative problem-solving has evolved since its inception in the 1950s. However, it is always a structured approach to finding and implementing solutions.

The creative problem-solving process involves creativity. The problem solvers develop innovative solutions rather than obtaining help to learn the answers or implementing standard procedures. The creative problem-solving process is at work anytime you identify solutions that have value or somehow improve a situation for someone.

Steps in the Creative Solving Process

The Creative Problem-Solving Process uses six significant steps to implement solutions to almost any kind of problem. The steps are:

- Information gathering, or understanding more about the situation before proceeding
- Problem definition, or making sure you understand the correct problem before proceeding
- Generating possible solutions using various tools
- Identifying the effectiveness of potential solutions before proceeding
- Identifying the best solutions
- Planning the next course of action
- Solutions implementation

CREATE AN IDEA RICH ENVIRONMENT FOR PROBLEM SOLVING

Innovation and freedom to explore, inviting new ideas are important for the problem-solving process. For the "think-tank" sort of ideas to grow, organizations need to put together teams of skilled high performers. High Performance is a gradual and incremental process. One may need to step back in order to step forward to evaluate new ideas, validation of something new may not have instant results, and organizations must be willing to invest time for the gradual process to manifest.

Key factors in exploring problem solving are:

- Clear understanding of issues, problem, or crisis
- Clarity of goals
- Clear vision

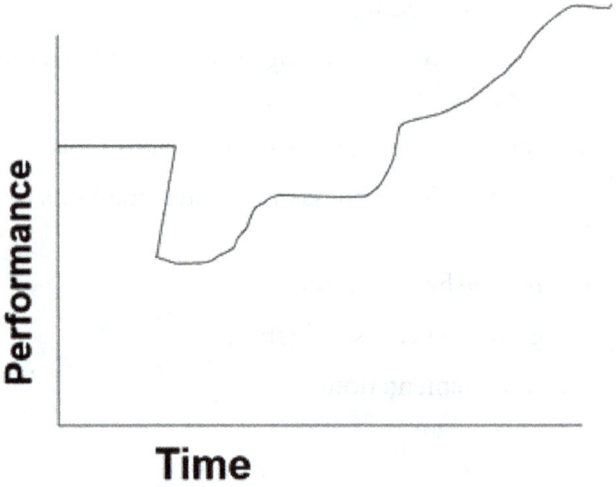

INNOVATIVENESS, EFFECTIVENESS, AND COMPETITIVENESS

We have noticed that, in this current phase of economic evolution, we are witnessing the outline of a new promise enabling sustainable development goals to be pursued simultaneously. In the past few decades, it has been evident that mass ideologies have disappeared, and the individual has been able to emerge.

Rather than focusing on ideology, it is now crucial to focus on an individual's development. The important thing is that people can be part of the 21st digital economy, not the ideology. Basic needs, health, human rights, social protection, and financial security place much higher than ideologies or doctrines.

Modern society has experienced such a paradigm shift as a result of advancing technology. This transformation demands setting aside our gender differences and being part of the new world of social innovation, economic growth, inclusion, and global diversity.

Next, individuals' ecological degradation and psychological disintegration are becoming increasingly high, and we are aware of the invisible costs of economic development. There is yet more to be assessed to compare the price of damage done to human civilizations and the earth's precious resources and progress made.

Ecological and psychological problems must be considered in the development of our economy. Greater good over mass production, depleting our resources, and damage to ecosystems and micro-organisms need immediate attention and damage control.

The younger generation needs the proper education, leadership skills, and resources to deal with challenges for the next two to three decades leading into the mid-century. The skills and tools used by past decades' leadership are insufficient now for the Fourth Industrial Revolution. This requires very different skills and youth perspectives.

organizations
belonging compassion authenticity
influencer thoughts inspiration
culture responsibility collaborations
enlightened humility purpose transformation,
strength power relationships
influence cohesive
freedom accountability courage
organizer
service stake-holders guidance
bravery connect conscious-business
clarity
self-worth self-esteem
self-mastery

CONSCIOUS LIVING, CONSCIOUS CONSUMERISM, AND CONSCIOUS LEADERSHIP FOR TOMORROW

In the year 2021, there were six generations in workplaces. A lot more effort and research are needed on how business, social entrepreneurship, healthcare, and service industries have to learn at different levels of needs based on the audiences they serve.

We mortal humans can only understand reality by considering our experiences through consciousness. Books and school do not teach us much about consciousness. We become conscious when we become aware. Leaders are similar to birds that take flight without any outside guidance. Due to its firmly rooted navigation system, the bird is able to do this. An individual who is equally rooted in his internal navigation system is also rooted in their consciousness, and they are able to make connections between their experiences and the coherences of that consciousness. In taking on the uncertainties of the outside world, leaders use this consciousness as their navigation system.

> *Leaders use their consciousness as their navigation system to take on the uncertainties of the outside world.*

Conscious consumerism is becoming more popular since the post pandemic, which brought our attention to take a pause, standstill, and observe the world around us. Investors and businesses are becoming aware of the preference of young people and their interests in eco-friendly choices. Following an EU research done on, "Strategies to Engage Millennials and Generation Z in Times of Uncertainty."

Four Pillars of Engaging Millennials and Generation Z:

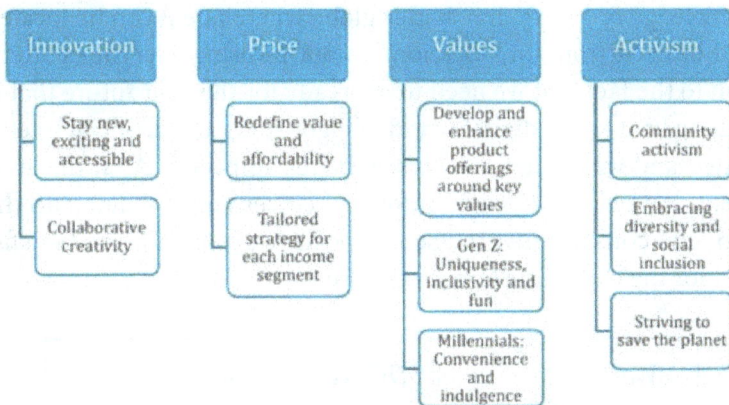

Innovation	Price	Values	Activism
Stay new, exciting and accessible	Redefine value and affordability	Develop and enhance product offerings around key values	Community activism
Collaborative creativity	Tailored strategy for each income segment	Gen Z: Uniqueness, inclusivity and fun	Embracing diversity and social inclusion
		Millennials: Convenience and indulgence	Striving to save the planet

IMAGE SOURCE: WWW.EUROMONITOR.COM

OUR WORLD AS A GLOBAL VILLAGE

There is a ripple effect created by every individual in creating the future. Learning to break old practices to allow new ones to emerge, we need to learn to let go of the past, live in the present, and prepare for the future.

The distant future, our humanity, and our aspirations as human race depends on the equality of life, unity of all, basic rights for all, clean air, and clean water for all, taking care of our beautiful blue planet and its resources. I recently heard the words of celebrities and Astrophysicists that, looking from space at our blue planet, there are no borderlines and boundaries visible from above. This brings to another concept of Vedic thought that "*Vasudha Kutumbhkam*" meaning earth is a family. My goal for this book to create awareness about our precious resources may be in danger and we have time to do something about it.

My focus remains on the need for creating awareness in our rapidly changing world that is quickly moving into a digital era, in a knowledge economy, in a flatter globe where talent can be located and utilized from any location. I want to bring everyone's attention to the fact that we need to get ready for the near future that is pulling us into the digital world of algorithms and artificial intelligence, and we are not able to see the full impact of AI at this moment. We need to become informed citizens and understand the pros and cons in order to use AI's positive powers for our benefits and for the overall sustainable future.

> *Working toward the SDGs can be meaningful and purposeful if we introduce persuasive aspirations for our communities.*

So many among us are living in the past while trying to live in the present through deliberate intent, but they're not in the present, not in the now. The participation towards sustainable goals must be from every level and everyone. Even small efforts can account for substantial changes for the benefit of many.

I often talk about managing polarities of thoughts and purpose and seeing a common goal in both. Having too many "good" goals at once becomes too much to handle. A goal must align with purpose and a sensible, doable (SMART) action plan. We need to evoke the kindness in our hearts and bring it to action!

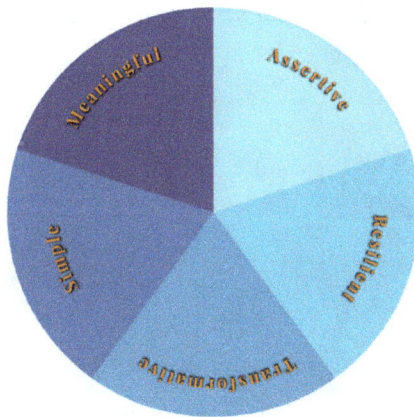

Ritu Chopra's Version for SMART Methodology

❙ SAGE ADVICE ❙

As we have moved through the generations, we need a different set of skills that suit our demands for the current circumstances, challenges, industrial and economic growth, environmental and public health challenges of the societies and nations. So, the need for leadership skills changes to adapt to lead, engage, and persuade, especially in the 21st century, in the age of technical advancements as we heavily rely upon instant communications, social media dominating the information distribution at a rapid pace.

CHARISMA & ADAPTABILITY OF A LEADER OF THE 21ST CENTURY

How to be successful at work or business or in life requires varied skills to suit your circumstances and environment. Finding the right team with the right skills, delegating, motivating, managing, grooming, and keep performing are imperative to professional success. Navigating the rough waters, and swimming with business sharks in high seas, managing expectations, mentoring, leading, and managing it all requires people-skills in addition to business knowledge.

THE PERCEPTION OF A CHARISMATIC LEADER

The answer to this question of who a charismatic leader is may not be easy. Leaders are not just defined by genders. If we look at the history of the world, especially the history of the women in the past 200 years, we can see unique characteristics of these outstanding leaders who in their own ways were very charismatic. We can see these leaders' world just not limited to politics or a specific industrial domain. Amelia Earhart, an aviation pioneer, was unlike any other woman leader of her time.

As I referred earlier to the research and study by *Heilman 1980; Heilman & Stopeck 1985*, physical appearance accounts for perceiving who is charismatic. In my view, anyone who has the courage to lead, regardless of their defined role, and create an example for others to follow, ally, and collaborate in the effort to bring the change, is a charismatic leader.

From an organizational point of view, creating a value-based, reward-based structure for the teams to get maximum output, the charisma, personal power, and adaptability of a leader is of utmost value. The timeless personal assets of integrity, accountability, and persistence are the key traits to empower those around you.

Adaptability

Adaptability often can be based on context described differently. However, some common traits of leader's adaptability are:

- Taking risks
- Managing risks
- Going outside the comfort zone
- Willingness to accept results
- Seeing the bigger picture
- Seeing other's point of view
- Changing with change

Leadership Qualities for Mid-21st Century

In this third decade of the 21st century, humanity is at the doorsteps of the digital world, and we must prepare ourselves and our younger generation for digital citizenship. Leadership for the future requires not just the key traits, or timeless values of leaders we have known strong leaders possess. The post-pandemic of COVID-19 in the last two to three years has changed a whole lot in how we view work and life, and how we buy products. It has only accelerated the change that was already in progress. At the verge of this change, and a flatter globe and global marketplace, availability of talent pools, and integrated economies, we must ask ourselves an important question: ***Are we prepared for the transition into the next few decades?***

My idea of seeing the world around us from a global perspective, not local or regional, brings me to explore the need for readiness for our future, our overall well-being, and the planet's resources to be available to us into the far future. Also, what we can contribute to the greater good from an individual level? As a strong believer of the efforts being put into the Sustainable Development Goals (SDGs), a lot of innovative solutions are being implemented, however at a smaller scale. I want to bring awareness to the fact that we all, at every level of the society, can bring about small changes. Women, at every level of the society and generational level, have higher empathy, a nurturing nature and can be the powerful sources to lead the changes given their abilities, resources, and interest. Our precious resources of the planet, clean air, clean drinking water, and food security are just the basic needs. The Digital World brings us many opportunities to prepare for, for example, education, learning, skills, and the future of workplaces.

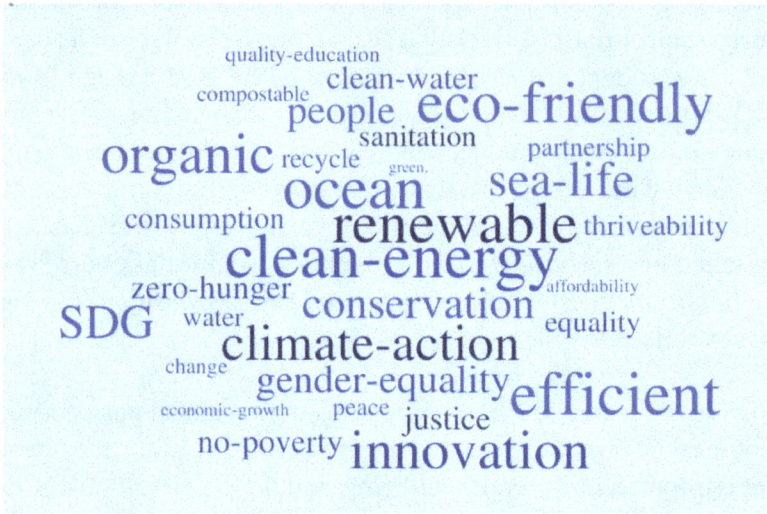

Let's discuss the future of work and youth perspectives. Today, in the early third decade of the 21st century, we have six generations in workplaces. Each generation, with their uniqueness, has experienced some common changes in just the last few years. COVID-19 pandemic had forced us to take a hard look at our readiness and adapting to unanticipated global events.

> *Currently, we have six generations in workplaces.*
> *Each generation with their uniqueness, has*
> *experience some common changes in just last few*
> *years.*

YOUTH PERSPECTIVES OF EDUCATION, LEARNING AND WORK OF FUTURE

Younger workforce, born between 1990 and 2005, suffered at much higher rates due to the pandemic affected losses of business and jobs. This is an age group of younger workforces, who are on the early career path of gaining skills. The rise of AI is another challenge this group has which have limited their opportunities in terms of skills needed for work. According to the Davos Lab Youth Recovery Plan report, which had survey results of youth from 180 countries, less than half were confident about their skills for the next 10 years. The concerns are not just limited to financial but also healthcare and related costs. More organizations now engage gig-workers and contingent workforce, leaving many people to plan for personal emergencies and costs.

Under such conditions, where there is a lack of skills of continuation or paid work, I wanted to address how do we prepare the Gen Zs for leadership roles for our educational institutions, governments, industries, and businesses. I found that a few countries, during the pandemic lock-down, used innovative learning platforms for early education of children, especially for the underprivileged families. These memories are very fresh for most families with young children during pandemic lock-down. Expanding on these thoughts of early education, the workforce readiness and talent pool availability in two decades from now will be different than even today.

Education, including early to higher education leading into skill development, many organizations are investing in the future workplace strategies of "Social Innovation" that is critical to the business growth.

> *As a technologist, I am in awe that how quickly*
> *our daily lives have turned in to the world of*
> *algorithms and bots from the palms of our hands*
> *to our doorbells.*

It seems that the intertwined challenges and solutions we see to-day, **frontier technologies** are leading the direction with artificial intelligence, robotics, and AR. As fascinating as they seem to be as a solution for humanity's future, there are many hidden dangers if not addressed and monitored by global governance. Staying on the solutions and productive side of these frontier technologies, we are able to explore the depth of the ocean, future of medicine, global health, and be part of the circular or digital economy. Which also means the skills we have today, will be obsolete for many jobs and work fields that lie ahead.

Digital Citizenship for Digital Literacy and Digital Economy

Digital citizenship basically refers to a responsible and sensible way of using online technology. A key component of digital citizenship is the ability of members to behave civilly and maturely online. Digital media allows us to communicate, collaborate, learn, and share online with others worldwide. When engaging with others online, we must ensure safety and security in the interconnected platforms and algorithms monitoring our behavior.

On the global platforms of our interconnected world, we have op-portunities to exchange ideas, seek information, and engage with other cultures different than ours. Communicating in online com-munities with people with high qualifications and talents is a priv-ilege to engage with. The level of connectedness that has developed over the last few decades has allowed us to communicate with people we may never encounter, share content and stories with audiences of all kinds, and access information, news, and media at our convenience. This is a great example of equality of thought sharing.

Equal access and digital skills become essential if we are going to utilize the most from our ever-expanding digital world. To make the digital age a more prosperous place for students, it is crucial to coordinate international efforts for education and training that would help them succeed in this age while minimizing the risks and inequalities associated with it.

Modern life cannot be imagined without the digital world. Communication, learning, shopping, and entertainment are all part of the world of social media. Connecting people across the globe is a transformative power of the digital world. What leadership qualities would you expect in others in our digital camps?

To maximize opportunities and minimize risks in the digital world, students should develop digital citizenship and a more comprehensive set of digital skills. A comprehensive understanding of the digital world can help ensure everyone has a voice in the future since the present generation will shape the future.

> *Digital citizenship must be inclusive. Ultimately,*
> *each of us has a role in the digital age.*

The most common nine elements of digital citizen outline the access, rights, responsibilities, communications etiquette, and legal aspects:

ACCESS – The level of access a citizen has varies. The goal of citizenship should be full access.

COMMERCE – Online shopping is on the rise, and it is important for consumers to know what they are purchasing and whether their purchases are legal.

COMMUNICATION – A citizen should make wise decisions about what and how he or she communicates online because there are numerous ways to do that.

LITERACY – Keeping up with digital changes is essential for technological literacy.

ETIQUETTE – Communicating with others requires etiquette as part of digital citizenship.

LAW – In addition to knowing the laws that govern them, citizens must behave ethically and responsibly.

RIGHTS AND RESPONSIBILITIES – Equal rights are granted to all users. There are responsibilities attached to these rights.

HEALTH AND WELLNESS – A lack of attention to ergonomics and other problems can lead to physical and psychological issues.

SECURITY – Protecting information online is the responsibility of citizens. Online presence creates digital footprints that may not be able to be erased.

Digital Literacy

Digital citizenship and digital literacy are intertwined, as digital literacy is the effective, ethical, and sensible use of technologies available to all users regardless of their identities and geo-locations.

> *Digital citizenship and digital literacy are intertwined, as digital literacy is the ethical and sensible use of technologies available to all users regardless of their identities.*

How would you define leadership roles or qualities in this new digital world?

Digital Identities

Online digital identities are collections of information about individuals, organizations, or devices. Individuals and devices can be identified by unique identifiers and usage patterns.

Digital Inclusion

More than a billion people have no legal identity per World Bank records. Seemingly, these people will have no access to financial services or resources. Digital identities begin to play an important role in identification and inclusivity.

So many benefits have been achieved with the use of digital identities around the world, not just in low-income nations but also in major cities in developed nations. Some of these include issuing digital health cards and biometrics to improve vaccine delivery in developing countries and for homeless people with a blockchain solution enabling access to healthcare, employment, and housing. Digital identity to increase inclusion, such as digital identity-based microloan platforms in least-developed countries and conflict zones.

All of this is indicative of the positive aspect of technical advancements. We are aware of the many dangers that technology poses alongside this tremendous benefit. The objective here is to provide opportunity, skills, and resources for all to participate in a new global digital village.

I want to bring you back here to the same question—the near future we are heading into, what do we need to prepare our youth for the right skills needed heading into mid-century?

What other skills or reskills requirements must organizations address to create the talent pool and future leaders of tomorrow?

What role can women play when given leadership opportunities as greater access to information becomes widespread?

How would you measure the charisma and adaptability of a leader when we see people in their most extreme circumstances are able to lift themselves up?

> *What does leadership mean to us going into our integrated digital world of new possibilities?*

Future Workforce and Employment Readiness

The key for future readiness is how we educate, skill, and shape our youth today. There has been tremendous progress in the education sector to go online in hurried ways due to COVID-19. Digital literacy provided continuation of learning to students in the early period of pandemic. Unfortunately, the downside remained for the under-privileged population without access to digital means.

In order to participate in labor markets of the near future, education and new skills for future work are integral parts of education systems. Lifelong learning pathways include gender equality, economic growth, behavioral and data sciences and more importantly social innovation. Social innovation in our future of work is critical in the long term, all environmental and social issues have financial impact to the economies and nations.

For organizations and businesses to include social agenda in their business model, has long term strategic benefits which can result in providing ways and means to low-income citizens to participate in the global economy. And how can organizations achieve this goal and what will motivate them to do so? Social innovation is not just for finding buyers, but future talent pools across the globe, reducing turnover costs, retention, and strategic placement for business continuity. Promoting the social innovation initiatives benefit all and is a win-win idea. After all, it is people who buy products or services. Without means and resources or lack of buyers, companies will also suffer.

So, the future of work is changing very fast right before us. Artificial Intelligence based technologies and tools are replacing human intervention and automation, identification of issues and troubleshooting can be done without human intervention. The roles displaced by AI tools are shifting the need for re-skilling or developing new skills for the digital economy. This seems too much too fast in the last couple of decades, comparing the growth that came at a manageable pace in the last century.

> *All living generations are impacted by the use of Artificial Intelligence.*

Future Technologies

The Fourth Industrial Revolution has triggered innovation in artificial intelligence, synthetic biology, and quantum computing. The advancement of technology is redefining human beings by pushing the limits of lifespan, health, and cognition in ways that were once the stuff of science fiction.

COLLECTIVE THOUGHT, COLLECTIVE RESPONSIBILITY

Consequently, individuals and organizations should take collective responsibility to foster innovation that benefits society. To respond appropriately to phenomena such as prolonged life, gene editing, and memory extraction, it is critical to address the moral and ethical issues arising from the new discoveries.

The biological domain in the innovative field creates many ethical issues regarding data privacy, health information, policies, and regulations, including rights and responsibilities for altering the genetic code of future generations. Data privacy and identity protection-like issues should be at the top of the agenda for policymakers and regulators as the new digital age is already here.

Too much is still unknown and undecided. So, to form any solid opinions for their cost, benefits, utility, and access for masses, dangers and downsides are very premature as we have a lot more to learn. However, the application of sensible policies and adherence to them, data privacy and security, and monitoring must be in place. The smart machines, with human-like qualities, create another set of challenges for human augmentations and their ability to autonomously make life-or-death decisions.

It's essential to ensure that this industrial revolution fosters humanity and enables technology to empower people and be a tool they can use. With the increase in online interaction, there is concern that people will become less able to listen, make eye contact, or read body language accurately as they become less accustomed to face-to-face interaction.

In addition, there has been growing concern that the Fourth Industrial Revolution negatively impacts social skills, such as empathy, as it intensifies our personal and collective relationship with technology. Value creation, exchange, and distribution have fundamentally changed due to the Fourth Industrial Revolution. We are experiencing an evolution in technology that combines the physical, digital, and biological worlds into one.

Artificial intelligence, genome editing, augmented reality, robotics, and 3D printing are some fast-evolving technologies driving it forward. This revolution also requires governing these solutions in a way that empowers, fosters collaboration, and helps build a more sustainable foundation for economic and social growth.

Fourth Industrial Revolution

It was in Great Britain, around 1830, that the First Industrial Revolution began. This led the farming communities cultivating land and handicrafts economy to large-scale industry, mechanized manufacturing. The Second Industrial Revolution, from the mid-19th century until the early 20th century, was primarily centered in continental Europe, North America, and Japan. Toward the end of the 20th century, the Second Industrial Revolution spread around the world.

The industrial revolution brought about widespread changes in economic and social structures, from agrarian economies to steam engines, light bulbs, assembly lines, and automation. Resulting in a broader distribution of wealth and international trade. Industrial organizations and their managerial hierarchies took shape to skill and oversee the division of labor.

The Third Industrial Revolution, aka the Digital Revolution, began in the 1970s. This digital revolution changed the mechanical and analog technology to digital computers and digital ways of record-keeping that we currently use. The internet and technological innovations have transformed conventional production and business techniques in our information age.

The **Fourth Industrial Revolution**, or **4IR** conceives rapid change to technical advancements in industries, social norms, and business processes in the 21st century due to growing interconnectivity and smart computerization.

Klaus Schwab, the World Economic Forum Founder, and Executive Chairman emphasizes that the term **Fourth Industrial Revolution (4IR)**, is more than productivity improvement. Drastic shifts and transitioning into digital economies require re-skilling and new skills for future jobs in most fields.

The 4IR comprises Artificial Intelligence and Advanced Robotics, shaping our physical, biological, and digital world in unimaginable ways.

We are witnessing fundamental shifts, continuous automation, and smart technologies changing how we live and work daily.

The technological growth and implementations of smart machines resulting in less human intervention, self-monitoring, analyzing, and resolving issues is a common scene. The digital age we entered in the 1990s and the virtual world we find ourselves in at present is another interesting aspect of our speculative future connectivity.

Leaders of Tomorrow

Whether the future leaders are men or women, both will need to be trained and prepared for skills for the future, and studies conducted post COVID-19 pandemic, which had brought up many changes about how we live and work, teach us that almost half of the working population may need re-skilling for future work in the digital and circular economy we have entered in.

The circular economies are sort of a "Win-Win-Win" model, and why shouldn't we embrace it? Circular economies reduce waste, reduce carbon emissions, and minimize the use of the planet's resources. Repairing, recycling, and redesigning products to keep them in use for as long as possible.

We are also witnessing the evolution of alternatives to shopping, practicing, and living; social media, virtual venues, e-sports, digital gaming, safe out-of-home venues, and social distancing pods for dining, exercising, and attending festivals are all examples.

▎ SAGE ADVICE ▎

Each generation perceives leadership with different measures and metrics. In our recent history, the nations have passed through significant challenges, some causing global, regional, and wide impact, while some remained localized to specific geographical areas. The expectation from the leaders to manage and resolve such challenges can be much different than a normal set of skills and leadership traits. People's expectations of their leaders change dramatically to lead us through the unique circumstances and challenges. Adapting quickly to lead, as situations demand, with charisma and poise sets apart the strong leaders who successfully lead through the crisis with the best possible outcome.

BELIEFS, VALUES & FUTURE OF THE PLANET

BELIEFS

It is often hard to express beliefs of nations, societies, and the rulers, which are so varied and so much centered on their ideas of power. However, if we think about humanity as a whole, we can bring our attention to common needs, goals, social protection and security, social justice, basic needs of food, health and education for everyone to participate and be part of the circular economy.

It requires participation from everyone, governments, educational institutions, businesses, and industries including people at all levels.

We must give ourselves an opportunity to assess small changes for the sake of our own future and for our younger generation to be part of thriving life experiences on the planet.

For many years, going as far back as my adolescence years, I recall being so curious and learning about other cultures and people and often took interest in reading folk stories from other cultures. Some of them have created greater curiosity to understand the purpose of our being here, in this vast galaxy of planets and stars. In the real world, the realities we come across are not just harsh or brutal, that many people are going through. Few of the precious cultural concepts, I quote here are:

- UBUNTU (I am because we are)
- IKIGAI (A reason for being)
- VASUDHA KUTUMBHKAM (Earth is a family)

Ancient cultures have given us the beautiful concepts of *ikigai*, *Ubuntu*, and *Vasudha Kutumbakam.*

I am always in awe of how much history has presented to us over the centuries, and all of these lessons are so relevant still in our modern era. Now a days, we have information at our fingertips, instant and available in every known language that we can translate just with the touch of a button in our handheld devices if we are curious about understanding the strength of these wisdom-filled concepts.

The concept of ikigai is to live a life using your passion, what you love, what you are good at, what you can be paid for, and what the world needs, seems to be more critical than ever as we are stepping into the Fourth Industrial Revolution of integrated economy, global economy and, let's say, the circular economy. All integrated tools, systems, and software can efficiently utilize global talent.

As the younger generations enter the workforce, the gig economy has sprouted with the talent these young people, the technology-savvy age bring to the table. There is a stark difference between them and their parents' generation, who were proud to stay with the same employers for decades, earned pensions, and retired from the same companies. It is now a phenomenon of the past. However, within a few short decades, the technical revolution has expedited our appetite for technological tools, gadgets, devices, household appliances, and cars. We have become more technology dependent. The changes we are experiencing due to the expansion of technology are undoubtedly life-changing, functional, and bring many advantages to our daily lives. On the other side, the labor markets that our parents' generations were familiar with have changed drastically. This means that with each new generation entering the workforce, we are experiencing very different organizational players, talents, tools, and strategies that are shaping the today's world.

As *Ikigai concept* explains that, "To be successful at what you do, love what you do, and you can use that as a trade that you could be compensated for," seems to fit today's marketplace more than ever. We can find passionate players and talents regardless of the geographical locations as technology platforms can now bring buyers and sellers into one integrated platform in the gig economy.

Quote from Hector Garcia's book, Ikigai, "We often think combining tasks will save us time, but scientific evidence shows that it has the opposite effect. Even those who claim to be good at multitasking are not very productive. In fact, they are some of the least influential people."

In the words of Aristotle, "We are what we repeatedly do. Excellence, then, is not an act but a habit."

One of the concepts of ikigai encourages how to turn the free time into spaces for growth. Next, going with the flow is also a big part of the ikigai concept. Your consciousness, body, and action are all united into a single entity, and you become completely immersed in the experience, not thinking about, or distracted by anything else. Your ego dissolves, and you become part of what you're doing. How often have you heard that, when we enjoy any activity, time vanishes and we lose track of time. That's precisely the concept of being dissolved, being immersed, going with the flow, and to do what we love to do.

The exciting fact about creating a flow or having a flow has nothing to do with a geographical location or cultural background. People anywhere can achieve the flow when focused on a concrete task without any distractions. The mind becomes focused and flows in order.

The challenge is that if the mind is on many other things and actions or not focused on, just the opposite will happen; in other words, there is no flow.

A researcher at DePaul University, Owen Schaffer, explains that the requirements for achieving flow are:

1. Knowing what to do

2. Knowing how to do

3. Knowing how well you are doing

4. Knowing where to go, where navigation is involved

5. Perceiving significant challenges

6. Perceiving significant skills

7. Being free from distractions

This model encourages us to take on tasks that we have a chance of completing, but are slightly outside of our comfort zone.

If the rules for completing a task or achieving a purpose are too primary relative to our skill set, we will likely get bored. Activities that are too fast or unfocused lead to disinterest. On the other hand, if we assign ourselves a task that is too difficult, and we don't have the skills to complete, we'll almost certainly give up when we feel frustrated. So, flow and balance both become essential part of achieving desired goals.

Japanese Proverb: "Fall seven times, rise eight."

In the modern world, many psychologists have taken up the concept of *Ikigai* as it brings the resilience part of us being human. The resilience of human beings can also be seen as *emotional resilience*. In this concept of *Ikigai*, pursuing passion is expected regardless of the many hurdles or challenges one may face. Resilience, then becomes more than the capacity to persevere and endure. It is also the attitude we can cultivate to remain focused on important things in life rather than what is most urgent and avoid being swayed into negative emotions.

IKIGAI: RELEVANCE IN MODERN SOCIETIES

Good health and well-being, ongoing physical and mental activities, and connecting with nature (*our precious resources*) are vital to the human experience. Especially in modern days, our lives have become complicated with an influx of technology, stressful routines impacting peaceful life experiences, and food products we consume which are often filled with chemicals that jeopardize our health. *Ikigai* concept remind us to find our purpose, creativity, and belongingness and stay active regardless of external challenges. Once we are in sync with our inner self, and know our goal, we can quickly adapt to external circumstances.

Vasudha Kutumbhkam

Vasudhaiva Kutumbakam is a *Sanskrit* phrase found in *Vedic* texts such as the *Maha Upanishad*, which means "The World Is One Family." Vedic tradition mentions "Vasudhaiva Kutumbakam," meaning all living beings on the earth are a family. (Source: **Wikipedia**)

Vasudha Kutumbhkam—What lessons can this uplifting thought present to us?

How does this relate to the world vision or future of humanity? As astrophysics and astronauts say, from above space, earth has no demarcations or boundaries. It is a beautiful blue planet.

Are we honoring the purpose of our creator that "Earth is family?"

The thought that earth is family does not reflect that all are the same and have the same ideas or understanding. Just as the members of a family have different levels of understanding, traits, values, beliefs, outlook, and capacity to perform, still they are tied to the family's roots. The thought of bonding, ties to roots, is more important than diversity of thought. The concept also can be defined as, "**Unity in Diversity.**" Our global diversity is now part of our modern economy. Nations and people are inter-dependent for exchange of goods and services across borders worldwide.

VASUDHA KUTUMBHKAM: RELEVANCE IN MODERN SOCIETIES

Given our current business landscape, we work with people across the planet via integrated technology across borders and time zones. I personally have experienced it in my professional career. So often we spend more time with our colleagues than with our own kin. As a curious person, I have been interested to know more about their culture, work culture, and things important to them, perhaps as a polite and professional gesture, others seem to be interested in getting to know us. Well, this is just an example. How often we have come across doctors, professors, and other professionals and interact with them despite our cultural differences.

More so, we have become interdependent on people worldwide for talent sourcing and providing goods and services, not only in mass from organizational distributions of services but as individual entrepreneurs as well. This was not possible before the technical platforms arrived to connect us across borders.

Ubuntu Emphasizes That Society Gives Human Beings Their Humanity

Per the dictionary meanings of the Zulu proverb Ubuntu, Ubuntu (Zulu pronunciation: [ùɓúntʼù]) is a Nguni Bantu term meaning "humanity." It is sometimes translated as, "I am because we are," (also "I am because you are") or "humanity towards others" (*Zulu umuntu ngumuntu ngabantu*). It's a way of living that begins with the premise that, "I am" only because "we are."

The Kenyan literary scholar James Ogude believes Ubuntu might counter the rampant individualism pervasive in the contemporary world. "Ubuntu is rooted in what I call a relational form of personhood, meaning that you are because of the others," says Ogude.

> "In other words, as a human being, you, your
> humanity, your personhood—you are fostered
> in relation to other people. People will debate,
> and people will disagree; it's not like there are no
> tensions. It is about coming together and building
> a consensus around what affects the community.
> And once you have debated, then it is understood
> what is best for the community, and then you have
> to buy into that."
> SOURCE TTBOOK.ORG, WIKIPEDIA

In short, what gives us dignity is not our independence but our interdependence, our ability to participate and share with one another, and indeed our vulnerability. This African and relational conception of human dignity has yet to influence many outside sub-Saharan Africa. I hope that this tribute might help in some way.

Desmond Tutu's ideas about humanness, harmony, and reconciliation have been enormously influential in South Africa and worldwide.

Scholarly references to Ubuntu and its equivalents go back to the mid-twentieth century. One of the most famously brief glosses of the term is that from the philosopher John Mbiti. For Mbiti, Ubuntu can be captured by the idea,

> "I am because we are, and since we are;
> therefore, I am."

Mbiti explained the concept like this: "Only in terms of other people does the individual become conscious of his own being, his own duties, his privileges, and responsibilities towards himself and others. When he suffers, he does not suffer alone but with the corporate group; when he rejoices, he rejoices not alone but with his kinsmen, his neighbors, and his relatives, whether dead or living." (Source: https://www.lookingforwisdom.com/Desmond Tutu, Ununtu, and Possibility of Hope)

UBUNTU: RELEVANCE IN MODERN SOCIETIES

This socialization is a vestige of agrarian peoples as a hedge against the crop failures of individuals. Socialization presupposes a community population with which individuals empathize and, concomitantly, have a vested interest in its collective prosperity. Urbanization and the aggregation of people into an abstract and bureaucratic state undermines this empathy. However, African intellectual historians like Michael Onyebuchi Eze have argued that this idea of "collective responsibility" must not be understood as absolute in which the community's good is prior to the individual's good. On this view, Ubuntu, it is argued, is a communitarian philosophy widely differentiated from the Western notion of communitarian socialism. In fact, Ubuntu induces an ideal of shared human subjectivity that promotes a community's good through an unconditional recognition and appreciation of individual uniqueness and difference. (Source: **Wikipedia**)

Collaborative Societies: How We Can Create Them

- Aspirations and ambitions—placing them at the right places
- Creating win-win for all—social impact
- Emotional Intelligence and Generational Intelligence

- Managing what you know and what you don't have much control of
- Accountability and Integrity
- Money and the Matters
- Managing roadblock

> *"Do not try to change the world, change your world."*
> —PROF. DR. WAYNE VASSER

VALUES BASED ON GLOBAL VISION

Values are essential, particularly in times of crisis.

As the fundamental beliefs that guide or motivate people, organizations, and communities, they provide a basis for social justice and belief in necessary institutions.

They also express personal and collective judgments about what is important, influenced by culture, religion, and laws.

Values can potentially spur purposeful action aimed at increasing equality, decreasing harm to the environment, and improving global health.

Creating "Conscious" Leaders of Tomorrow: Re-thinking of Crisis Today

Requires understanding the skills needed for future leaders. Education, learning, and trade skills leading into the future of work, employing the neuro-divergent, under-privileged and providing every one opportunity to be part of the global economy.

BASIC AND DEVELOPMENTAL EDUCATION

The development of technology as an integral part of educational materials, distribution of educational content, and evaluation of educational outcomes occurred even before the pandemic.

While some education systems have made significant progress in incorporating even the simplest learning technologies, particularly widely available ones, some systems need more time.

As a result of inequalities in technology access, online education efforts have suffered during COVID-19. As much as some have viewed technology as an effective means of addressing issues related to unequal access to education, especially among traditionally marginalized groups and those living in rural and hard-to-reach areas, the pandemic highlighted the need for additional infrastructure to address these issues.

When WHO declared COVID-19 a pandemic, and a few months after, UNICEF reported half the population in 71 countries did not have access to the internet for remote learning as of mid-2020.

Social Innovation

WHAT DOES SOCIAL INNOVATION MEAN?

"Social entrepreneurship is described as not just an activity, but it stands for a mindset. So, with this mindset, we can see it is now penetrating business and governments as well as the educational system."

—Hilde Schwab, Co-Founder and Chairperson of the Schwab Foundation for Social Entrepreneurship

Social issues are not new to corporations. To participate in the global economy, billions of low-income people need access and opportunities. Increasing social innovation means being more ambitious, strategic, and collaborative. A wide range of corporate governance tools, corporate philanthropy, and corporate social responsibility tools have been used by companies for many years to exercise their citizenship in society. *To ensure a just, sustainable, and equitable world, social innovators work hard to find systemic solutions to overcome the world's most pressing problems by developing systemic solutions.*

As a result of this approach, social innovation differs from traditional techniques in that it pursues societal challenges in a way that creates tangible benefits for the business itself. Social innovation strategies share certain features, despite their differing methods and techniques:

A direct alignment between the company's innovation agenda and its business strategy is achieved through these initiatives. We can see some significant factors for business strategies to include social innovation in the business models. These strategies utilize a company's core assets to gain a competitive advantage:

- Organization Human Capital
- Value Chains
- Technology
- Distribution system

The main operation or business unit of a company manages them. These companies will benefit from financial returns and improved long-term competitiveness, including access to new markets or consumers, strengthening supply chains, and retaining talented employees.

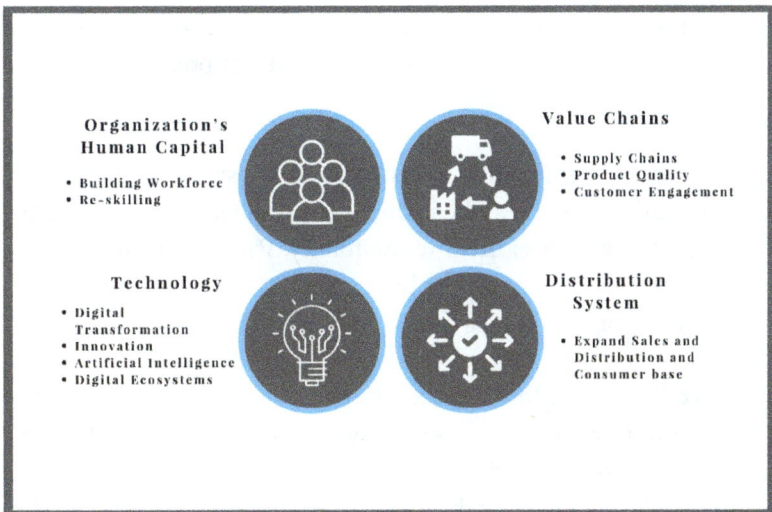

EXACTLY WHY DOES SOCIAL INNOVATION MATTER TO BUSINESS?

> *"It is society that gives us the right to be active, our license to operate. A business leader has to think about how to solve the societal challenges of today, because if we don't solve them, we will not have a business."*
> —PETER BRABECK-LETMATHE
> CHAIRMAN OF THE BOARD, NESTLÉ

For businesses to earn stakeholder trust and retain their license to operate, they must be able to enhance their net positive contributions to society.

We anticipate significant challenges that most societies globally will face in the decades ahead include the lack of access to education and healthcare, income inequality, widespread unemployment, and environmental problems such as climate change and ocean pollution, to name a few.

It has been proven, through experience, that government policies alone cannot provide solutions. However, partnerships with businesses of all sizes—creating and distributing products and services domestically and across national borders—are needed to develop social innovation.

It is no longer possible for business leaders to focus solely on financial results and profits as the main driving force to determine the company's destiny.

Over the last few decades, philanthropy has evolved into corporate social responsibility and social innovation has become a major component of corporate engagement. Social problems are addressed more long-term through sustainable social change rather than one-time projects.

Rather than being a solo project, it represents a strategic direction. We need to develop solutions that will enable those traditionally excluded from participating in economic growth at grassroots levels and beyond.

So, we can see that the driving force behind social innovation is the long-term purpose, partnership with communities, and accountability on their part to continue to focus on the future of the planet and humanity in focus. Developing social innovation is driven by a sense of purpose, a sense of partnership, and a sense of accountability.

Essentially, it is the process of creating or improving products, services, business models, and markets so that they can more effectively respond to the unmet needs of global citizens and thus solve global problems.

The scale of social enterprises' impact depends on the collaborative efforts of business, government, and civil society across boundaries.

WHAT ARE THE BUSINESS BENEFITS TO PURSUING SOCIAL INNOVATION?

> *What if the innovative technologies start conspiring against us?*

Economic Progress and Challenges

ESG skills and capabilities are defined in following sectors as:

- Banking and capital markets
- Future of the environment
- Economic progress
- Corporate governance
- Data science
- Artificial intelligence
- Sustainable development
- Education skills and learning
- Enterprises and employment

Equality and Inequality

The effects of conflict on women and girls differ from those on men and boys. Displacement and breakdowns of protection services expose women and girls to more significant risks. It is estimated that 70% of women and girls are exposed to gender-based violence in crisis situations. Such circumstances increase the likelihood of child marriage in many regions, even in modern times.

Inequalities in the structure of society mean that more women die from disasters such as droughts, floods, and storms than men. It is often difficult to identify and meet the requirements of women and girls in the aftermath of disasters, and their specific humanitarian needs are often neglected following disasters. To add to the list are unwanted pregnancy, STDs, and maternal mortality, unhealthy living conditions, lack of basic amenities. This can significantly hinder women's education, paid work, and physical and mental well-being.

While research shows that women's participation in crisis response and prevention can improve outcomes and lower the risks, this is doable. Women and girls must be involved in planning and implementing humanitarian action, focusing on their rights, needs, and agency.

It's important to note that the COVID-19 pandemic has contributed to income inequality and exacerbated health inequality, age and disability inequality, gender inequality, technological access, infrastructure, and geographic location inequality, especially for women in underprivileged communities. The recent pandemic has been an eye opener for societies small or large, organizations, governments, educational institutions and health organizations.

Social and economic systems that aggravate inequality must now be changed both bottom-up and top-down to mitigate inequality.

We still have lot of work to do to improve the living conditions of women and provide them with basic needs and dignity in many parts of the world. As their contribution to the economies can not be ignored, it is only to our advantage to create an equal, fair, and dignified place for women.

Social Entrepreneurship

Entrepreneurial social enterprises produce socially and environmentally positive impacts and financial returns by solving problems innovatively.

It is becoming increasingly common for entrepreneurs to inject a social mission into their companies. These social enterprises, by utilizing market-based mechanisms, also provide self-sufficient innovative solutions to significant issues. Social enterprises tend to place a social mission at the core of their business while maximizing resources to achieve maximum impact.

Social entrepreneurs are often unique among traditional entrepreneurs in that they can sense opportunities and act on them by applying creative thinking to transform them into opportunities. There is huge opportunity for women who have been inspired by STEM programs, and having the background and expertise from their long career in Corporate arena, to start social or cause based enterprises. Thus, contributing to their family's income, providing employment, and contributing to economy by participating in social cause, the create a win-win scenario. The social entrepreneur's commitment to disrupting the status quo by generating social impact at a massive scale distinguishes the social entrepreneur from others.

OUR MISSION FOR FUTURE

Global Health and Preparedness for Future Pandemics

We are experiencing global demographic shifts, environmental pollution, and climate change impacting humanitarian crises where poverty is a significant barrier to achieving global health. All these forces are driving change differently, from technological innovation to an increasing global commitment to healthcare as a right.

We are also witnessing the new ways of improving global health which are emerging in partnerships with the private sector. As health, poverty, and sustainable development become increasingly interconnected, international governing bodies and multi-stakeholder partnerships are recognizing the relationship. There is still much effort required to respond to future pandemics and global health crisis. The need to protect and improve global health, prevent communicable diseases, track and respond required concentrated efforts from many different sectors from the communities including NGOs and humanitarian agencies.

Poor health and lack of proper preventive care, undermines the proper physical development, education in early years for many young people globally. In the age of precision medicine and bio-technologies available to us, my hope is to see organized efforts in place to prevent future pandemics.

Sustainable Development Goals: Where We Stand

SUSTAINABLE DEVELOPMENT GOALS (SDG) are the United Nations' declaration and plan of action for people, planet, and prosperity. Moreover, it aims to contribute to the strengthening of universal peace through greater freedom. A new universal agenda for the development of the United Nations is evidenced by the 17 Sustainable Development Goals and 169 targets.

At the core are the 5 Ps:

- People
- Planet
- Prosperity
- Peace

- Partnership

To tackle some of our most pressing issues, the Sustainable Development Goals (SDGs) of the United Nations provide an architectural framework. As you see the graph below, the 17 Goals have been defined to achieve multiple goals and targets people and planet. It is crucial that we change the way we work, produce, and consume.

Additionally, it involves addressing longstanding problems like poverty, particularly its effects on young people. We must address these issues with bold solutions and creative thinking for future generations.

To accomplish this, increased cooperation and a focus on sustainable development are needed. We must listen to the communities most affected by inequality and implement environmentally friendly policies to prepare us all for future emergencies.

During the COVID-19 pandemic, SDGs progress was hampered by small businesses' disproportionate suffering during the pandemic. Small and medium-sized enterprises (SMEs) are essential for achieving the United Nations' Sustainable Development Goals because they can contribute to economic growth and job creation by effectively sustaining them.

Increased participation from women entrepreneurs is evident in the post-pandemic period, due to disruption in labor markets and many having to leave jobs to care for family members and young children.

GRAPH SOURCE: HTTPS://SDGS.
UN.ORG/2030AGENDA

We are at a critical stage, where we have increased use of artificial intelligence, global platforms to seek and procure talents, Cyber-security, and Global Governance issues, moving into the Fourth Industrial Revolution that brings its own unique challenges of Digital Economy, Geopolitics, Climate Crisis, Systemic Racism, Global Diversity and Inclusion, Food Security, Humanitarian Crises, Social Innovation, Social Protection, Global Health, Educations, Skills and Learning to name a few.

> *Let's come together to create a better future and strong leaders for tomorrow.*

Corporate Social Responsibility (CSR)

In the third decade of the 21st century, we see in the business world, corruption, greed, conflict, competition, monopolization and in our societies during the explosive and troubled times, violence and terrorism and the value of human life diminishing every moment. Our current state of affairs seems to be in a chaotic stage, let alone influenced by the profit centered business organizations' greed.

In the globalization, the gap between rich and poor has gone up. It has changed the concept of our values in the way we see people. Though they are consumers, the quality of life hasn't gotten much better in this century, given that we have so much advancement made in terms of food, medicine, and consumer products. The process that's involved in the food production, is not at its best for human health. The cost of medicine for common treatments is outrageously high and unaffordable. Distribution of basic medicine for common diseases that can be easily treated is not available to communities who need them the most. Who do we blame, other humans?

We are reduced to the state of chaos, uncertainties, conflicts, greed, environmental threats, terrorism or possibly bio warfare. We don't want to say that no one is paying attention, or nothing is being done.

Few of those who are making remarkable effort to continuously bring light to such disasters or upcoming monumental challenges are definitely acknowledged. However, that is just a drop in the bucket. So much more action is needed, awareness is needed, and not just the nonprofits, few kind hearts, or a random CSR program is enough. We are at the doorstep of environmental disasters. The

global competition has complicated our lives with economic crises, family life crises, many environmental hazards, and human
health impact. We hear about business ethics, corporate social responsibility. It is not misstatement karma, however, the average
person's life quality and the gaps between the rich and the poor
have increased due to the high costs not in just terms of the money
or the cost of living, but in the declined quality of life of the average family.

There were certain practices in many ancient cultures that rulers
were taught and adhered to which remain timeless advises for the
leaders of any generation who are leading the organizations in our
modern-day society. These values were founded for the organizational leaders or leaders in any role in the society to be mindful,
compassionate, flexible, honest, and to serve with sense of service
to humanity. We don't see that too often, yet the practice of today's
leaders are seen to be in self-interest or profit oriented. That does
not mean these values have disappeared, they do exist and there are
conscious leaders who want to lead with such values. Their honest
and sincere interests for serving their consumers and prospects are
influenced by the shareholders value and become profit-centric.

Corporate Governance

Corporate governance is more than looking out for the interests of
stakeholders and customers or employees.

The Governance mechanisms, regulations, and corporate adoption, defining corporate purpose, risk mitigation, global diversity
and inclusion, social justice, sustainable development, and many
other factors play a role in the Fourth Industrial Revolution (4IR).
In the digital world and global economies, cyber-security, capital

markets, supply chains, Artificial Intelligence, and agile governance are a few other critical factors to consider.

CULTIVATING TRUST AND INTEGRITY

Companies must establish a trust to succeed long-term. To establish trust, individuals must maintain integrity and put the interests of their organizations (and society) before their own. Creating a culture of mutual trust through responsible corporate governance is possible. This requires transparency, confidence, and accountable leadership.

RISKS AND RESILIENCE

Many types of risks can have devastating consequences for any organization, including operational, financial, technological, environmental, and regulatory risks. Managing all types of current and foreseeable risks is an essential element of effective corporate governance.

First, risks must be prioritized, and here the board of directors can play a key role by deciding in what priority they should be addressed, what is to be deemed simply unacceptable, and how they should be addressed from a structural perspective.

It takes collaboration among the different parts of an organization to implement a robust risk management system, including the board's risk committee, internal auditing, finance, legal, and operations.

Environment, Social and Corporate Governance (ESG)

Societies today cannot have organizations and companies that destroy the world and then put band-aids on what they destroy. It's no longer acceptable; it's destructive, not sustainable as humanity faces a multitude of challenges in next few decades. A lot of organizations are likely responsible for earth's environment and destruction.

So, the only way for all organizations, or for us as women, as citizens of this world, to voice to the organizations that the whole entire global village has to take responsibility. In other words, we as women leaders, must convey to the organizations that we, as a global village are responsible to take care of our planet.

As the saying goes, it takes a village to raise a child. If the global village is responsible for protecting the planet and raising its children with dignity, then we must think about what is an organization? What is a corporation in today's world? Is it allowed for the corporation to destroy the planet and then put band-aids?

We need United Women to call on the global community to say we need to rethink how we organize our life human life on this planet. We must reorganize all our relationships with each other and our planet, and how we manage and define organizations now is destructive. We can't have it first destroyed and then put band aids on it.

ı SAGE ADVICE ı

Looking back at 200 years of human history, every few decades marked significant progress the civilization made in social, agricultural, economic, and industrial levels. The beliefs and values of leaders of the past have definitely set the foundation for our generation to build upon. However, our unique challenges are different than a century ago, and require a new set of skills, value system based on humanistic values to serve the public interest.

MANAGEMENT STRATEGIES, TOOLS, AND TECHNOLOGIES

A research study done by Bridgeworks, provides some insight into generational names in various countries within the scope of their research project. As we see our generations and people in the contexts of the events taking place in the respective regions, the perception of leadership traits, values and skills can be packaged accordingly.

USA	INDIA	CHINA	RUSSIA	BRAZIL	UK
Traditionalists	Freedom Fighters	Post 30s/ Post 40s	Silent Generation	Traditionalists	Silent Generation
Baby Boomers	Free Generation	Post 50s/ Post 60s	Sputnik Generation	Baby Boomers	Baby Boomers
Generation X	Generation X/ Generation E	Post 60s/ Post 70s	Gen X/ The Last Soviet Generation	Generation X	Thatcher's Children
Millennials/ Generation Y	Generation Y/ Generation E	Post 80s/ Post 90s/ Little Emperors	Generation Y/ Generation Pu	Generation Y	Millennials

Each generation brings its own view of the world. Which can be seen as opportunities and threats to businesses. This creates a great need to prepare each generation for the workforce a bit differently especially in the era of high technology, Automation and Artificial Intelligence.

Now, as mentioned earlier we have arrived at the doorsteps of our future world of education, learning, skilling, to live with artificial intelligence, Virtual and Augmented, peek into the digital and circular economies, corporate led initiative for social innovation, circular business models, urbanization, future cities, global governance, global diversity, social justice, human rights, sustainable development goals, biodiversity, environments and oceans all being an integral part of the Fourth Industrial Revolution.

What is needed, assessing the gaps, and how well we are equipped with the tools and resources available today to shape our future.

WORKFORCE AND WORKPLACES OF TODAY

Management experts used to think that management decisions were purely secular and objective. They had no subjective cultural element involved when they made decisions regarding the company's management. A work culture's ethos and essence must be understood to make successful business decisions today since management is about motivating people.

To spread our civilizational branches forward, we must also look backward and inward and establish deep roots in our spiritual culture so we can look forward into the future. We gain wisdom from understanding our past and history. Understanding our civilization's past is a collective intelligence of how we approach life's challenges in the future, both known/anticipated and unknown.

Creating wealth and economic movement is the outcome of all the efforts of individuals, families, societies, and nations. Every system, whether democratic, monarchical, or capitalistic, depends on wealth. Wealth and future economic stability require the participation of capital, labor, land and resources, technology, and other resources.

In business, how men and women communicate and interact has dramatically changed. During the past few decades, our roles, conversations, and expectations of each other have changed. But our disagreements, disconnect, and differences have remained, including the generational mindset.

As more and more men and women occupy the same workplaces and leadership roles, the conflicts and differences among the genders are ever-present. Due to the increasing number of men and women occupying similar positions of authority and corporate leadership roles, there are more and more conflicts and differences between the genders' views and visible perceptions of the matters.

It is not a doomsday situation but an opportunity to understand the gaps and create better communication between themselves. Here we have a lot of work to do.

> *The situation isn't doomsday but a chance to better understand one another and promote better communication.*

Impact of COVID-19 Pandemic

WORKPLACE JOURNEY

COVID-19 pandemic continues to reshape work cultures around the world. These trends will continue to reshape for various reasons as per the industries; talent pool availability, labor costs, and workplace distance are among the top reasons. Employers have struggled to get employees back after strict lockdowns have been lifted. The workers, before the pandemic lockdown, worked from job locations, successfully worked remotely, and found that work-life balance was better. Others on the career path may find it harder to connect with peers and seek higher roles. At the same time, employers were struggling to bring the worker back, and "great-resignation" took many employers off-shore to find remote workers at lesser costs.

Talent and the right skills are other critical factors for employers to seek needed skills for switching roles due to innovations or other reasons. The influx of issues here is another reason we must attempt to explore the required skill sets for the near future and re-skill if the current skills will become obsolete. This shift may take time to settle or may be a dynamic shift for quite some time as robotics and AI keeps taking over. It takes a while to identify skill gaps, and time for training and re-skilling can add up. As more and more Human Resources organizations turn to Digitalization and predictive analytics, there are still many gaps that a data-driven decision can solve. However, it is an attempt in the right direction. Digital know-how is essential for future success, and the time to invest is now.

WORKER'S JOURNEY: Existed regular traditional jobs, Great Resignation, Quiet Quitting, Re-skilling, these terms became global.

The Fourth Industrial Revolution significantly impacted livelihoods, generating severe demand for new skills.

A report by PwC shows that in the UK alone, AI and innovative technologies will eliminate approximately 7 million jobs by 2038. Around the same time, another 7.2 million new jobs will be created in the healthcare sector, education systems, and other scientific industries.

Historically, new skill sets have been fostered through decades of building training systems and labor market institutions.

We must develop more effective ways to help people develop new skills and halt job losses as we anticipate the magnitude of this technological disruption.

We cannot afford to sit back and wait for employers to implement training and learning systems and train the workforce. This will impact the income and earnings of individuals. We must educate ourselves about the skills needed for upcoming decades, proactively explore where our current skills and interests align, and prepare ourselves.

Of course, the business must do its part to see where the most impacts will occur and must offer re-skilling and occupation transition. Local or regional labor laws may also provide guidance as applicable.

> *Corporations need to look at People & Planet first and PROFIT later.*

"*From an execution perspective, we will always need head-driven leadership skills, and when we can add capabilities that provide; trust, psychological safety, and emotional intelligence to the balance, things get even better. While EQ has recently become one of the more dominant topics of discussion amongst leadership teams (and rightfully so) we can't forget about the operationally driven mindset and what it accomplishes in the workplace.*"

—Monte Pedersen

> *Our personal journeys are on the cusp of fear to faith and everything in between. We need not compete with others but try to overcome our own fears. Be the best we can be.*

❘ SAGE ADVICE ❘

Industrial revolutions of the past century have given us strong foundations, growth, innovations to continue. Work ethics, business strategies, techniques of innovation of past generations following World War I and II created a foundation for our generation to expand and advance innovation in new industries. In the beginning of the 21st century, we seem to be living in a Global Village with integrated economies, information technology, and artificial intelligence being part of our daily lives. The rapid changes we have witnessed in the last two to three decades are mesmerizing. And the rest of the third decade will bring more changes at a rapid pace with AI and Robotics into our daily lives and work.

FUTURE OF THE ORGANIZATIONS & SHARED VISION

CRISIS TO CONSCIOUSNESS

The shared vision for the future is to include innovations in every field for the benefit of everyone and harmony with nature while integrating technology into our daily lives.

We need to do our part to take the lead in making small changes for the future of our generations and the planet. We need leaders at every level in these societies, communities, and institutions of all sizes, not just in the large organizations, for our sustainable earth, resources, and safe living conditions.

For a global village to care for our planet, our future, and the well beings of the habitants of the earth, we must look at human strengths, resilience, and desire to take conscious action for humanity's future to create and raise conscious leaders of tomorrow.

INNOVATIONS IN ALL FIELDS AND DOMAINS

Why is this important or even relevant for leadership topics?

I see leadership as a combination of qualities that anyone can apply and lead others around them. We have seen young teenagers become leaders on the global stage, for example, Mallela Yosef, Greta Thunberg, and Boyan Slat. Leadership is not limited to specific corporate or organizational roles. These young people are perfect examples of leadership icons and beacons of hope.

The younger generation between the ages of 18 to 24 is making a significant impact on consumer markets by creating awareness of how economic behavior impacts our planet's resources. The COVID-19 pandemic had touched multiple segments of our lives, and it took its toll in unimaginable ways. It has changed how we live and work, choose to move around, spend our money, our time, and the impact of the production of these products causing it to peel the environment. As we can see, the younger generation of consumers are conscious consumers, and they have the power to exercise a positive influence.

The focus we can see on the purchasing power of the younger generation directly involves how corporations and organizations need to concentrate their efforts on business transparency and decarbonization of supply chains, including climate actions while seeking governments to implement policies and regulations. All stakeholders must come together to achieve such results and make the change possible. The World Economic Forum published the *Davos Lab Youth Recovery Plan in 2021*; due to the COVID-19 pandemic, young consumers and investors are leading the efforts to achieve climate and social justice. In 187 countries surveyed for this report, young buyers want policies encouraging sustainable consumption while penalizing non-sustainable production.

Awareness of the impact on the planet's limited resources, and making sustainable choices, is our civic duty at this time. Women as caregivers, while raising young children, have many opportunities to instill conscious consumption habits and adopt the same practices in the household. This responsibility is NOT limited to young mothers; every conscious citizen, man, or woman of all ages, must participate in this effort.

The global population is constantly shifting due to many reasons for people to migrate, either from war-zone areas, refugees, or due to seeking employment are some top factors of changing demographics. Other factors are climate change, loss of agricultural land due to natural disasters, or political issues. These demographics create another challenge and humanitarian crisis for the healthcare of the impacted population. Health issues directly affect people's ability to work and be productive. Costs of healthcare follow where some basic healthcare amenities may be available.

CONCLUSION

Many studies prove that women leave leadership roles due to family commitments and raising children. I have spoken with many highly educated women in responsible roles and (observed), over time, women have delayed childbirth. This is primarily due to the highly stressful career, travel, or long working hours, financial stability, including their ambitions to rise higher in their career path.

Even then, women have to prove their worth over and over again. Unfairly, expected to put in more work than their counterparts. Lack of support, mentoring or coaching, and training organizations often not designed to fit to assist women leaders.

Please consider the reports on why women leave leadership roles. The most critical reason shown in the studies is family requirements. That, too, proves most working women take added responsibility of raising a family, and managing household duties, alongside the demanding responsibilities at work. I want to remind you that women, as nurturers, put us last while doing everything else. We often forget to nurture ourselves. For so long, I felt guilty taking time for myself and doing something for myself. I have heard the same from many of you, putting everyone else before us.

My question is: we are leading all this effort against many odds; who do we need to tell us that we have leadership qualities? In my view, leadership is not limited to a job title. Remind yourself that the nurturer, being "you," is of a high value you give to other human beings, and this commitment to "give" more than receiving is a quality worthy of leadership values. Don't we expect leaders to be kind, caring, and compassionate?

Aren't we already doing it (in unpaid work, without corporate titles)?

Why shouldn't these qualities be considered worthy of leadership?

Corporate leaders so often lack these values that we expect from them in leadership roles.

I looked at and researched the history of women's contributions, struggles, sacrifices, rises, and successes for the past 200 hundred years from many cultures and nations around the world. We have given women the power and respect of being Goddess; on the other extreme, they have been trafficked, tortured, and abused for man's pleasure. Like any other human, women are not free of shortcomings and sabotage against other women. However, that is comparatively a smaller number of women who have been aggressive and behaved so coming from insecure positions.

My attempt here is to bring our attention to the fact that we have accomplished a lot in the last 50 years, worked against our own DNA, paid a high price to prove our worth, and are still demanding an equal place in society in the 21st century. I ask you to instill pride in yourself and the glow of being the power that resides within each of you. As givers of lives and nurtures, the bigger responsibility we have been given, know that you have the qualities of being a leader, listening, caring, and mentoring your young children, who will be the leaders of tomorrow (boys or girls) who grow up as men and women, makes us a part of the family, both men and women are an integral part of the society, we cannot be independent of each other. I ask you, the women of the world, to know your power and that you are a valuable part of the family, community, and our culture, with or without a title given to you by any job.

For all men, please look around and think about how many women have contributed to your success. Honor them for their contribution to take you in shiny spotlights. These women are not just in your workplaces, but mothers, grandmothers, aunts, teachers, and many more who contributed to giving you the opportunities to rise. It is only fair to ask to be treated with respect and equality.

Where we stand now, in this third decade of the 21st century, there is no way to go back to our past. The future needs contribution from each and every one of us, no matter how big or small. Men and women must come together to face the challenges humanity faces. We need collaboration, not competition; we need to see the rapidly changing world around us with open eyes.

In every report I've read in my research in the last two years, no matter whether published by any International Organization, NGO, Business entity, Educational institution, or a major Data or Statistics resource, one thing in common I found is that each of these reports has COVID-19 pandemic reference and went on what shifts the pandemic has forced upon us in their scope of the research studies or whitepapers. So many talented men and women around the world I interviewed had something important to share about the drastic challenges they had experienced in their work, business, or industry due to the pandemic. The aftermath is still fresh in our memories, and the world has not recovered from the damage caused by the COVID-19 pandemic.

It has changed how we work, learn, school, and many other social norms. COVID-19 has been a big equalizer in how nations worldwide have seen irreplaceable life loss, not to mention financial and economic losses.

My focus is on how we prepare ourselves as one humanity, save our precious resources, create conscious leaders of tomorrow, and be the leaders in leading our next generation into a better world. A world of human dignity and respect, preserving our precious and limited resources, ecosystems, biodiversity, earth, oceans, and clean air for the health of all living beings. There is so much we need to pay attention to now; away from competition and greed, come together with kindness and a well-being mindset for all life.

We must set aside the gender wars and biases that no longer serve us in our future journey. We must see from a refreshed outlook that the new "digital" world has pulled us into its grips, and there is no looking back, only forward and to the future. It is time to come together and design the future to be better, safer, secure, healthier, and abundant to support the needs of all life. People and the Planet before Profits!

> *"Know that we have the power to endure the change, to bring change within our hearts is even more powerful. We dare to manage and lead ourselves through adversities and rise. Leading and managing ourselves are the qualities of a leader, no matter at which stage of life you are. Be successful, be victorious, and be amazing!"*
> YOURS TRULY, RITU CHOPRA

❚ SAGE ADVICE ❚

It seems that we are on a bridge between the present and future, and each bank around the bridge is so far apart in how we lived thus far in this century and how rapidly it is about to change. Let's make this change a positive one in every aspect of the new era, as much as we can by our conscious thought, living, consumption, human dignity, social justice, protecting resources, and decarbonization. I hope the thoughts and ideas presented in this book will provide readers to take actions where they can align themselves with causes or initiatives they prefer.

ABOUT THE AUTHOR

RITU CHOPRA, a technologist by profession, is an author, TV show host, award winning film producer and Executive Coach. With more than two decades in IT operations in Fortune 500 companies, Ritu now mentors and coaches emerging leaders to achieve their "Personal Mastery."

As president of Chopra Management Services, Ritu is a creative force, motivational speaker, and certified leadership coach with personal projects that are part of her commitment to giving back to the community. She wrote "Art of Life" and "Mastering Life" focusing on personal mastery to achieve success in professional domains. Her recently released title is *Women Leadership in 21st Century* and releasing soon *Magic in Mindfulness*. Ritu hosts and executive produces "Despite the Challenges®," a TV show, and "Women of Power" Podcast. As an executive coach and keynote speaker, Ritu also leads seminars and workshops to suit a variety of audiences and topics. Ritu brings her passion, humility, and dedication for inspiring her clients to engage their heads and hearts in clarity and creation. She has lived her life adopting her eastern philosophies.

TESTIMONIALS

The importance of creativity and innovation cannot be overemphasized in enhanced performance in the twenty-first century. I recommend this book as a great enlightening experience for leaders in a fast-changing world.

Ibilola Amao, PhD. FEI FNSE FIoD FAEng.
STEM/TECHpreneur

The book, *Women Leadership in the 21st Century*, gives you a glimpse into our rapidly changing world. Alignment with male professionals who endorse and participate in female equality—in addition to business deals and work—is vital. Ritu emphasizes the skills of tomorrow's leaders and a fresh look at how we all need to come together to create our new society.

Martin CJ Mongiello, MBA, MA, MCFE
The United States Presidential Service Center

This is a very informative and timely book, creatively designed to benefit both women leaders and entrepreneurs to understand the concepts (theories) assisted through practical examples of leadership, career development, personality development and empowerment.

The most significant contribution is that the book is published in the most critical time preceding COVID and made more accessible using practical experiences. It will help Women gain the skills required for decision-making needed urgently in the current and future context of societal transformation and emerging new social norms. At the end of the book, a clear and excellent attempt is made for women to realize how SDG 5 can contribute to achieving other SDGs.

Dr Renuka Thakore
Founder, Global Sustainable Futures
Progress through Partnerships Network
Global SDGs Women Ambassador

With a world seemingly spinning out of control, the need for leaders of today is vital. So, where can we find them? Author Ritu Chopra says those leaders can be found in the very first place we ever looked for guidance, our mothers.

Anthony Knopps
President of Strategic Communications, United States
Presidential Service Center

In current uncertain times, it is so important to create a clear understanding of the history of women in order to move forward on today's choices. In Ritu Chopra's book, she has carefully captured and presented both the facts and feelings that underpin a new female leadership ready to face the challenges of a fast-changing digital world. This book proposes a wonderful journey ahead when we are empowered to be in harmony together. Thank you, Ritu.

Dr Pauline Crawford, PHD
Entreprenology, The Conversation Game Changer

Every culture has a different approach about giving women the recognition they deserve. However, In most cases gender bias prevails and men are placed at a higher level. As a global society, we should study the practice of the elephants. The oldest female leads the herd. As more women are taking key leadership roles, we can see more equitable distribution based on knowledge and performance. Still, we have a long journey ahead of us.

This book aims not only to clarify misconceptions but to open dialogues that address issues that can be resolved only by actions. It is up to each individual to take the challenge and find ways to fight for the solution.

Dayci Chivukula
Master of Arts

Women have a key role in the nourishment and growth of new generations. Women are a symbol of bravery, courage, strength, and fortitude.

With the passage of time people developed extraordinary skills but women are still struggling with the same issues which she faced 100s of years ago.

Today's women have the solutions for the challenges we can foresee. I am happy that today's women are taking charge to solve the problems the world is facing, and are playing an active role in the implementation of sustainable Development Goals in every walk of life. This book brings together women of all generations together in a way to firm new partnerships by showcasing their contribution.

Ghazala Khan
Diplomatic Ambassador (FIGHR)

Ritu chronicles the struggles, biases, and successes of women and girls, from historical, professional, authentic, and thought leadership perspectives, whilst also infusing it with the depth of her experience and expertise, as an industry expert, mentor and entrepreneur in a way that calmly ushers the reader into the core of her message in the book.

Oluneye Oluwole
Founder, Story Chest Group Inc. Canada

Ritu Chopra has a way of digging out bits of information that can be turned into gold for the audience. Her insightful approach to women and leadership now and in the future helps to bring the subject to our minds in a new way; sometimes by way of paradigm-shifting. We will look through Ritu's lens and that of the women she utilized in her book as the foundation. I was so pleased to be included in her research, and look forward to learning from other women who are moving mountains and leading as role models in the bid for equality. The challenge before us as women, young or old, is to get to our center place—that place of knowing who we are and operating with confidence from that point no matter the circumstance. Ritu's book will help us find the path to that place.

Mary Kurek,
President & CEO / Frontrunners Development, Inc

Ritu G. Chopra has written an extraordinary book on how important it is to raise conscious "organic thinking" leaders, both men and women can learn much from this fascinating study. Highly recommended for emerging and seasoned men and women executives who need to level up to face the leadership challenges of the post COVID era and beyond."

Jody DeVere
CEO, AskPatty.com

Ritu's book illuminates a subject in an in-depth, yet an easy read for everyone without any indictment on anyone group. Her book paints a picture that depicts the state of women's role in starting with early civilizations. My word is that change is here, and this book helps rush it along.

Now, the doorway is open to a different kind of leadership not just for women, but for the world. Just imagine leadership not being a conversation of the "best man" for the job. We would cease to do double takes each time a leadership position is filled by a female whether it be on a local level or a world level. This book should be required reading for young adults.

Geneva McDonald

As a woman in the position of teaching sales techniques to other women, I often encounter a great deal of what Ritu speaks of in this book. Sales, in the past, was considered a "man's job." Women are often hesitant to appear too aggressive when selling their products or programs and it effects their income. We must rethink gender norms when it comes to work force and work skills. Women can become fantastic at sales often because of their gentler nature and powers of persuasion once they are given the confidence to move into their power. This book addresses so many relevant topics and is a must read for both women and men.

Jess Reidell
Ageless Jess Coaching